The Song of the Lord

BHAGAVADGITA

❖ Wisdom of the East Series ❖

The Song of the Lord

BHAGAVADGITA

Translated with introduction and notes by
Edward J. Thomas, *M.A., D.Litt.*

Charles E. Tuttle Company, Inc.
Boston • Rutland, Vermont • Tokyo

Published in the United States in 1992 by
Charles E. Tuttle Company, Inc. of
Rutland, Vermont & Tokyo, Japan, with editorial offices
at 77 Central Street, Boston, Massachusetts 02109.

Library of Congress Catalog Card Number 92-61873

ISBN 0 8048 1812 6

This is a facsimile edition of the work originally published in London by John Murray in 1931.

PRINTED IN THE UNITED STATES

CONTENTS

PAGE

Introduction 9

I. The Despondency of Arjuna . 25

II. Sānkhya 31

III. Action 41

IV. Knowledge 47

V. Renunciation of Actions . 53

VI. Meditation 57

VII. Knowledge of the Lord. . 63

VIII. The Lord as Brahma the Imperishable 67

IX. The Royal Knowledge and Secret 72

X. The Lord's Vastness . . 76

CONTENTS

		PAGE
XI.	The Lord as All Forms . .	82
XII.	Devotion	90
XIII.	The Field and the Knower of the Field	93
XIV.	Distinction of the Three Constituents	98
XV.	The Lord as the Highest Person	102
XVI.	Distinction of the Godly and the Ungodly	105
XVII.	Distinction of the Three Forms of Faith	109
XVIII.	Renunciation	113

EDITORIAL NOTE

WHEN the Wisdom of the East Series first appeared in the early part of this century, it introduced the rich heritage of Eastern thought to Western readers. Spanning time and place from ancient Egypt to Imperial Japan, it carries the words of Buddha, Confucius, Lao Tzu, Muhammad, and other great spiritual leaders. Today, in our time of increased tension between East and West, it is again important to publish these classics of Eastern philosophy, religion, and poetry. In doing so, we hope the Wisdom of the East Series will serve as a bridge of understanding between cultures, and continue to emulate the words of its founding editor, J. L. Cranmer-Byng:

> *[I] desire above all things that these books shall be the ambassadors of good-will between East and West, [and] hope that they will contribute to a fuller knowledge of the great cultural heritage of the East.*

INTRODUCTION

THE *Bhagavadgītā*,[1] the "Song of the Lord," has been called the New Testament of India, but for the history of religion it is more than that. It tells us wherein generations of Hindus have found and still find their ethics, their spiritual consolation, and their beliefs about God and human destiny ; but it also offers answers to many of the ethical and religious questions that are rife in the West, and the parallels and contrasts between the two worlds of thought are equally striking.

The literary setting is one of great interest. The Song begins with the problem of a conflict of duties in concrete form. It is an episode in the great epic of the *Mahābhārata*, the chief theme of which is the battle between the five sons of Pāṇḍu and their cousins the Kurus, the sons of Dhṛitarāshṭra. When the battle was about to begin, Arjuna, one of the Pāṇḍus, stopped his chariot in perplexity. As he was of the warrior caste, it was his duty to fight, yet he was fighting against friends and kinsfolk, and even against the

[1] The fuller title is *Bhagavadgītā upanishadaḥ*, "secret teachings sung by the Lord."

revered teachers of his youth. He did not even know whether it would be best if his own side were to conquer. The reply of Kṛishṇa, his charioteer, is the great principle of the Upanishads: the soul is indestructible. It neither comes into existence nor dies, and when it passes to a new life, the wise do not grieve. Arjuna's duty as a warrior is to fight regardless of consequences.

This was probably the whole of the original episode of the epic, and as such it forms a dramatic and fitting incident. But it has been developed into a discourse, the Lord's Song, giving a complete system of ethics and religion. It adopts the teaching of the Upanishads about the one reality behind all appearances, as well as the doctrine of periodical creation, or emission and reabsorption of the universe by the One.[1] It also adopts and applies the teachings of the current philosophies, but it interprets all their doctrines in a particular way. The One is no longer an impersonal ultimate in which consciousness and all differences disappear, but a personal being, who has become incarnate on earth as Kṛishṇa, and who is conceived as having such a nature that he is an object

[1] The doctrine of one ultimate origin of the universe first appears in the Vedic hymns. In the latest parts of the Vedas (Brāhmaṇas and Upanishads) the conception is developed, and the One is conceived as emitting the universe from himself and reabsorbing it. Creation is thus periodical, but it is not creation *ex nihilo*.

of love and devotion to his worshippers. This is the significance of the Song. It succeeded in incorporating into the brahmanical system the type of emotional religion which expresses itself in devotion (*bhakti*) to a personal God, and which finds its longings satisfied in love towards him. Of this the Song is the earliest and still the greatest monument of Indian religion.

The worship of Kṛishṇa originated in the west of India, and independently of any brahmanical influence. It became fitted into the established brahmanism by identifying Kṛishṇa as an incarnation of the Vedic god Vishṇu. It is a probable view that Kṛishṇa was a real person and hero of the Yadu tribe,[1] who became deified. He is not mentioned in the earlier Buddhist writings, though Vishṇu is, and this would seem to be a reason for putting the origin of the religion not earlier than the third century B.C.; but this is a fallacious argument. Religious developments may have gone on for centuries in the west of India without any contact with the semi-brahmanised regions of Magadha and Bengal. The Song represents so clearly an attempt to present the cult of Kṛishṇa in harmony with the teaching of the Upanishads and brahmanical ritualism that it is not necessary for its comprehension to try to fix its exact date. Although it speaks of those who

[1] Yadu was an ancestor, and Kṛishṇa or anyone of the tribe might be called Yādava, "descendant of Yadu."

do not worship Kṛishṇa, it makes no reference to particular antibrahmanical systems like Buddhism, but this only shows that it was not in close contact with them. Professor Belvalkar has recently tried to place it in the century before Buddhism, and certainly it appears as the direct development of upanishadic thought, as interpreted by a devotee who found this teaching realised in the divine Kṛishṇa. It is sufficient for our present purpose to say that it is later than the great movement represented by the early Upanishads, and earlier than the period when the orthodox philosophic systems were expounded in sūtras.

Attempts have been made, notably by Garbe, to dissect the Song on the supposition that it was once a purely theistic work, to which portions representing the teaching of the Vedānta system have been added. But his view that in this way it is possible to arrive at an earlier form of the poem has not been generally accepted, and we may confine ourselves to an analysis of the thought of the poem as it stands.[1]

The first part of the Song (I–VI) is ethical. It expounds what a man ought to do, not merely as a social being, but what his action should be in view of his ultimate destiny. This is found in the

[1] There is an excellent account of the various theories of the composition of the Song in E. Lamotte's *Notes sur la Bhagavadgītā*, Paris, 1929. Professor Belvalkar's views are given in his *Shree Gopal Basu Mallik Lectures on Vedānta Philosophy*, Poona, 1929.

doctrine of *dharma*. The word *dharma*, as expressing the ideals of action to which an individual should attain, may be translated "righteousness." It is "right" as opposed to wrong-doing (*adharma*), and in so far as it expresses the course of action that should be followed it is "duty." But it is duty which is wider than mere morality, for it includes all ritual laws and caste rules. The existence of caste, the theory that society is composed of certain distinct classes each with its own hereditary functions, introduces a further difference from Western ethics, for each class has its "own duty" (*svadharma*). But the teaching of the Song is much more than this. In spite of the survival of earlier conceptions, the ethical doctrine of the Song is among the most enlightened in the world. It opposes materialism and sensuality, not by setting up an ascetic standard impossible for the ordinary man, but by showing how the highest ideals of action may be followed, while all the duties of daily life are being carried out.

Kṛishṇa after reassuring Arjuna by pointing out that the soul cannot be killed, exhorts him to perform his duty, which, as he is a warrior, is to fight (I). But in order to do his duty properly he must do it with the right motive. All action should be done not for the sake of some personal advantage, but out of devotion to the Lord. The best way to acquire the power of doing this is by the practice of Yoga, a method of training the intellect so that it becomes detached from all external objects (II). In that case, Arjuna asks, why does Kṛishṇa enjoin action ? The Lord explains that no one can entirely refrain from action. Arjuna should perform his prescribed action, not for personal gain, and not led by the passions. This is the Yoga of action. The entire universe, according to the ancient Vedic conception, is a sacrifice, and the whole is kept going by the due performance of every part. Hence the ritual view of sacrifice is justified, but not if performed for personal gain (III, IV).

Complete renunciation of the fruit of action is difficult for those leading the ordinary life of men, and hence the method of training by Yoga practice is recommended. In this way complete detachment from worldly things is attained, and rules are given for the practice. But even one who cannot control his mind and detach himself reaches a world corresponding to his merits, and he may even be reborn in a family of Yogis (V, VI).

The second part (VII–XII) gives the theology of the poem. As the Lord is Nature, he is all the visible world, but through his higher nature he is the life-principle of all things (VII). He is the cause of all, and embraces with his vastness all existences. In Chapter XI divine sight is given to Arjuna, and he has a vision of the whole universe as forms of the Lord. The devotees may worship in different ways, but those with faith in the Lord are the best.

The remaining chapters (XIII–XVIII) deal with more technical questions of ethics and philosophy—on the distinction between the self and Nature, the character of those in whom each of the three constituents prevails, on knowing the supreme Person, on the godly and ungodly, on the three kinds of faith, and on the true meaning of renunciation and duty.

The Philosophy of the Song

All Indian philosophy is at the same time theology and religion. Each system is not a mere theoretical scheme, but is also a way of salvation. Common to all Indian religious systems are the doctrines of transmigration and *karma* (action), the view that every action receives due recompense in this life or another. The Upanishads had already taught the doctrine of one reality, Brahma, with which the individual soul is identical. But the relation of this reality to the world of sense remained a problem, and later schools, all appealing to the Upanishads, answered it in different ways. According to one of the schools of Vedānta everything but Brahma is illusion (*māyā*), and nothing but Brahma really exists. But in the Song *māyā* preserves its older meaning of the magic power of a god, his power of deluding.

Most of the Upanishads teach extreme pantheism, according to which the individual soul, the *ātman*, is identical with Brahma, and the task of the worshipper is to realise the identity. But several Upanishads, such as the *Maitrāyaṇa* and *Śvetāśvatara*, recognise a personal Lord, who is in some sense the All. It is this mitigated pantheism which is held by the author of the Song, and its direct connection with this teaching is shown by actual quotations in the Song taken from such Upanishads. The pantheism of the poem is thus fundamental. The great addition made by the Song to the upanishadic teaching is the introduction of the worship of Kṛishṇa. The burden of the whole poem is Kṛishṇa as the one refuge, and love and devotion to him as the means of salvation. With this as the basis, the author identifies the Lord with Brahma, the One, the Beyond, and he adopts the Sānkhya theories of the nature of matter and the external world.

Whether he has really harmonised all these views is a question to be considered, but if in his eager propaganda to win worshippers he has not made a consistent system, that is no reason for supposing that the teaching is not the fervent utterance of one man. As will be seen below, the contradictions that have been alleged are largely due to supposing that the philosophical conceptions introduced are those of the classical philosophies, which we have no reason to think were in the mind of the author, or even in existence at the time.

The Song teaches a means to approach the Lord. It is the practice of training and concentrating the mind called Yoga, and this too is found along with pantheism in the Upanishads. The *Maitrāyaṇa Upanishad* (vi, 17, 18) says:

This which is in the fire, that which is in the heart, and that which is in the sun is One. Verily to the oneness of the One he goes who knows this. The method of practising it is thus: restraining of breath, withdrawal (of the senses from their objects), meditation, fixing (of thought), reflexion, concentration. These six parts are called Yoga.[1] By means of this:

When one who sees, sees him of the golden colour,
The Maker, Lord, Person, Brahma, the Origin,
Then he who knows, forsaking merit and evil,
Makes all things one in the Supreme, the changeless.

Here we have three of the fundamental doctrines of the Song: the oneness of the All, the teaching about a Lord, and the means of approaching him by the practice of Yoga. What the Song adds to this is the doctrine that the Lord is Kṛishṇa.

The Yoga taught in the Song is not the philosophy of that name, but a method. Yoga is literally "yoking," and refers to the yoking or training of the mind so as to control the attention

[1] Classical Yoga gives eight. It substitutes *āsana*, "posture," for reflexion, and adds *yama* and *niyama*, certain moral rules and restrictions.

and all the mental activities, as explained in Chapter VI. The disciple must avoid bodily excesses, whether of indulgence or austerity; he should go to a place free from external distractions, choose a convenient seat, regulate his breathing and fix his mind on one point. He then becomes trained (*yukta*), and detached from all desire for the fruit of action. This is the Yoga of meditation (*dhyāna-yoga*), in which the recluse renounces all action as far as is proper and possible. The Yoga of action (*karma-yoga*) is the state in which the disciple practising detachment continues to live in the world and perform the actions due to his position, but with abandonment of the fruit.

Yoga is not union with God, but a physical and mental practice, which by cutting off external hindrances, and then controlling and training the mind, makes that union possible. Here we evidently have the type of religion known in the West as mysticism. To belief in a God hidden from the senses it adds the teaching that by means of a process of training the veil can be pierced, and union with him attained. It is also Indian belief that by the practice of Yoga supernormal powers can be acquired, clairvoyance, levitation, etc. But these powers do not aid in reaching the goal, and they are ignored in the Song, except in so far as they are implied in the reference to the deluding power of Kṛishṇa as Lord of Yoga (cf. VII, 25; IX, 5; XI, 4).

The Song explains the outer world according to the Sānkhya philosophy. Unlike the Vedānta, which recognises only one ultimate self, Sānkhya holds that souls are many, and that they remain for ever separate. And besides souls there is another ultimate substance, Nature (*prakṛti*). It is conceived as being at first (between two creations) undifferentiated matter with all its constituents in equilibrium. As such it is the unmanifested (*avyakta*). It is as the evolution of this Nature that all mental and material phenomena are explained. Nature has three constituents, *guṇas*, literally "strands of a rope." They are not qualities of something else, but the ultimate elements of Nature, which by appearing in different proportions produce the variety of actual existence. As forms of matter they are lightness (*sattva*), movement (*rajas*), and heaviness (*tamas*). But they are the constituents of mental phenomena also, and then they appear as goodness, passion, and dullness or stupidity. The soul (*ātman*) or person (*purusha*) is the permanent entity behind all the changes of conscious life. In classical Sānkhya the end of man is to free this self, or to realise that it is free, from all contact with Nature. This teaching about the end is also the doctrine of the classical Yoga philosophy, but it differs from Sankhya chiefly on two points. It has adopted the Yoga practices, and it has reintroduced the idea of a God, though this God is not the Brahma of Vedānta nor the all-embracing Lord of the Song. He is not even the creator, but a special soul, whose body consists only of the goodness constituent, and who acts as a kind of providence in helping souls to their goal. In classical Sānkhya, however, there is nothing beyond the two principles, souls and Nature. There is no oversoul or supreme Lord.

Evidently, this last point is not the teaching of the Song, and it is here where other contradictions have been found on the supposition that the author was trying to harmonise his teaching with the classical Sānkhya doctrine. But we have no right to assume that the author even knew the classical form. What he says contradicts the classical teaching, but he does not necessarily contradict himself. The Sānkhya as taught in the Song is the natural science of the time, and is independent of any philosophical theories that may lie behind it. The theory in the Song that lies behind it is that the Lord is all. Hence the Lord is also *prakṛti*, Nature, as well as the soul of the whole.

The real problem of the composition of the Song is not whether every part is consistent, still less whether it is consistent with later philosophies, but whether its doctrines could have been taught by one man. The tendency of modern criticism is in favour of the unity of authorship. There remain certain irregularities and repetitions, which make it probable that there have been additions, and this is also suggested by the circumstance that it has exactly 700 verses, but these facts do not affect the question of the real unity of the Song. There is a Kashmir recension in a MS. of the British Museum, which has fourteen additional verses and four half-verses. Dr. Barnett hesitates to accept them as genuine, and they are too few to affect the general conclusion.[1]

The worship of Kṛishṇa has diverged into a number of religious forms, and has followed different lines of development. Certain sects have tended to an eroticism which in India itself meets with reprobation. The chief movement has been in the direction of extreme emotionalism, in which the love of God is the sole means of salvation. Of Chaitanya (the great Bengali reformer, contemporary of Martin Luther) we are told that "his whole life was a passionate flow of love for this deity, and this emotion was generally so intense that as he sang and danced like a mad man he often became unconscious."[2] Yet though the

[1] See F. O. Schrader, *The Kashmir recension of the Bhagavadgītā*, Stuttgart, 1930.

[2] S. N. Dasgupta, *Hindu Mysticism*, Chicago, 1927, but Chaitanya (or Gaurānga) is held by the Vaishnavas of Bengal to have been a manifestation of Kṛishṇa himself; see note on IV, 8. For the history see R. G. Bhandarkar, *Vaiṣṇavism, Śaivism, and Minor Religious Systems*, Strassburg, 1913. Professor G. B. Mallik's work, *The Philosophy of Vaiṣṇava Religion*, Lahore, 1927, is an able and elaborate study from within of present doctrines.

vairāgī, the one who has renounced all worldly ties, still exists, the religion is predominantly that of the ordinary man, and it remains one of the greatest of the religious phenomena of India and of the world.

NOTE ON THE HISTORICAL SETTING

In Book VI of the *Mahābhārata* begins the account of the great battle, probably a real event of prehistoric times, between the sons of Dhṛitarashṭra and the five sons of Pāṇḍu, who had been cheated out of the kingship by their cousins. The sons of Dhṛitarāshṭra are called the Kurus in contradistinction to the Pāṇḍus, though, as the table shows, they were all descendants of Kuru.

- **Kuru**
  - **Śāntanu**
    - **Bhīshma**
    - **Vyāsa (stepson)**
      - **Dhṛitarāshṭra**
        - **Duryodhana and ninety-nine other sons**
      - **Pāṇḍu**
        - **five sons :** Yudhishṭhira, Arjuna, Bhīma, Nakula, Sahadeva

King Pāṇḍu was dead, Dhṛitarāshṭra was blind, and the power was in the hands of Duryodhana. The battle lasting eighteen days was fought on the plain of Kurukshetra (in the neighbourhood of the modern Delhi), and the Kurus were defeated. Dhṛitarāshṭra was kept informed of the fighting by his charioteer Sanjaya, who through the favour of

Vyāsa, the traditional author of the *Mahābhārata*, received divine vision to see it all. The whole of the Song is given as Sanjaya's narrative. The words "Sanjaya said" indicate the narrative portions. The words "Arjuna said," "the Lord said," imply that Sanjaya is reporting their words.

Other characters are, among the Pāṇḍus:

Chekitāna, an ally.
Dhṛishṭadyumna, son of Drupada.
Dhṛishṭaketu, king of the Chedis.
Draupadī, wife of the five Pāṇḍus.
Drupada, brother of Draupadī.
Jayadratha, king of Sindhu.
Kṛishṇa, of the Yadu tribe, charioteer of Arjuna and incarnation of Vishṇu.
Kuntī, wife of king Pāṇḍu.
Kuntibhoja, an ally.
Pṛithā, a name of Kuntī.
Purujit, an ally.
Śaivya, king of the Śivis.
Sātyaki, a name of Yuyudhāna.
Saubhadra, son of Arjuna.
Śikhaṇḍin, son of Drupada.
Uttamaujas, an ally.
Virāṭa, king of the Matsyas.
Yudhāmanyu, an ally of the Yadu tribe.

Among the Kurus:

Aśvatthāman, son of Droṇa.
Droṇa, teacher of the Kurus and Pāṇḍus.
Karṇa, king of the Angas.
Kṛipa, king of the Panchālas.
Saumadatti, king of the Bāhīkas.
Vikarṇa, a son of Dhṛitarāshṭra.

Epithets and names of Kṛishṇa: the epithets are usually not descriptive but allusive, and refer to incidents in legends about him. In translation they would be cumbersome. Madhusūdana (slayer of the demon Madhu), Arisūdana (slayer of enemies), Govinda (herdsman), referring probably to his being brought up with the cowherds, Vāsudeva (son of Vasudeva), Yādava (descendant of Yadu), Keśava (having fine hair). Others are of disputed meaning, such as Hari, Hṛishīkeśa, Janārdana, Mādhava.

Epithets of Arjuna: Bhārata (descendant of Bharata). Bharata was an ancestor of the Kurus and Pāṇḍavas (sons of Paṇḍu), and the name Bharata might be applied to any one of the race. Arjuna is frequently called Bharatasattama (best of Bharatas). Dhananjaya (winner of wealth), Guḍākeśa (having the hair in a ball). Other epithets, like Pārtha (son of Pṛithā), are translated.

THE SONG OF THE LORD

I

THE DESPONDENCY OF ARJUNA

Sanjaya informs the aged Dhṛitarāshṭra of the beginning of the battle, and tells him how Duryodhana, leader of the Kurus, describes to his teacher the warriors in the two armies, how the Kurus blow their conchs, the sons of Pāṇḍu reply to the challenge, and the battle begins, how Arjuna stops his chariot, and explains his perplexity to his charioteer Kṛishṇa.

DHṚITARĀSHṬRA said: Assembled on the field of right, the Kuru field, eager for battle, what did my people and the sons of Pāṇḍu do, O Sanjaya?

Sanjaya said: Prince Duryodhana, when he saw the sons of Pāṇḍu drawn up in battle-line, then approached his teacher,[1] and spoke:

"Behold this mighty host of the sons of Pāṇḍu, O teacher, drawn up by the son of Drupada, thy wise disciple.

[1] This was Droṇa. He was teacher to both the Kurus and the Pāṇḍus, who had been brought up together at the Kuru court.

Therein are heroes, great archers, equal in fight to Bhīmạ and Arjuna—Yuyudhāna. Virāṭa, and Drupada of the great chariot ;

5. Dhṛishṭaketu, Chekitāna, the valiant king of the Kāśis, Purujit, Kuntibhoja, and Śaivya the hero ;

Yudhāmanyu the brave, Uttamaujas the valiant, Saubhadra, and the sons of Drupada, all with great chariots.

But know those that are the chief of our side, the leaders of my army, O best of brahmins. For the sake of naming them I tell them to thee :

Thyself Lord, Bhīshma, Karṇa, Kṛipa, victorious in battle, Aśvatthāman, Vikarṇa, and Saumadatti likewise ;

And many other heroes for my sake renouncing their lives, with various weapons and missiles, all skilled in fighting.

10. Insufficient is this force of ours, guarded by Bhīshma ; but sufficient is their force, guarded by Bhīma.

So therefore, arrayed in your respective ranks, it is Bhīshma whom ye all must guard."

To raise his spirits Bhīshma, the eldest of the Kurus, the grandsire, the valiant one, sounding high a lion's roar, blew his conch.

Then the conchs, the kettledrums, the drums, the tabors and the horns were suddenly beaten. There was a roar of sound.

Then standing in their mighty chariot yoked with white steeds, Mādhava and the son of Pāṇḍu blew their divine conchs.[1]

15. Hṛishīkésa blew (his conch called) Pānchajanya. Dhananjaya blew Devadatta. Vṛikodara of terrible deeds blew the mighty conch Pauṇḍra.

King Yudhishṭhira, the son of Kuntī, blew Anantavijaya. Nakula and Sahadeva blew Sughosha and Maṇipushpaka.

The king of the Kāśis of the mighty bow, Sikhaṇḍin of the great chariot, Dhṛishṭadyumna and Virāṭa, Sātyaki the unconquered,

Drupada and the sons of Draupadī, and Saubhadra the mighty-armed, severally on all sides blew their conchs.

The sound rent the hearts of the sons of Dhṛitarāshṭra; even through earth and sky the roar resounded.

20. So Arjuna, son of Pāṇḍu, whose crest was an ape, seeing the sons of Dhṛitarāshṭra arrayed, when the fall of weapons was beginning, seized his bow,

And spoke thus to Hṛishīkeśa: "Between the two armies stay my chariot, O firm one,

So that I may behold them standing, eager for

[1] Mādhava is Kṛishṇa, and the son of Pāṇḍu is Arjuna. In the next verse they are called respectively Hṛishīkeśa and Dhananjaya. Vṛikodara (wolf-bellied) is an epithet of Bhīma.

the fray, these with whom I must fight in the battle that now begins ;

And that I may look upon them gathered here, eager for fighting, and wishful to please the evil-minded son of Dhṛitarāshṭra in battle."

Sanjaya said : Hṛishīkeśa thus addressed by Guḍākeśa (Arjuna) stayed the best of chariots between the two armies,

25. In the face of Bhīshma, Droṇa, and all the world-rulers, and said : " O son of Pṛithā, behold these assembled Kurus."

The son of Pṛithā saw standing there fathers, grandfathers, teachers, uncles, brothers, sons, grandsons, and companions ;

Fathers-in-law and friends in both armies. Beholding all these kinsmen arrayed, the son of Kunti,

Moved with deepest pity, spoke in dejection : Arjuna said : As I see these my people, O Kṛishṇa, arrayed eager for battle,

My limbs fail, my mouth is parched, trembling comes upon my body, my hair stands on end ;

30. My bow Gāṇḍīva slips from my hand, my skin burns, nor can I stand, and my mind is in a whirl.

I see adverse signs, O Keśava, nor do I find any advantage if I slay my people in battle.

I wish not for victory, O Kṛishṇa, nor kingship,

nor pleasures. What is kingship to us, Govinda? What are enjoyments or life itself?

They for whose sake we desire kingship, enjoyments, and pleasures, stand here in battle, abandoning life and wealth;

Teachers, fathers, sons, and grandfathers also, uncles, fathers-in-law, grandsons, brothers-in-law, and other kinsfolk.

35. Them I wish not to slay, though they are ready to kill, not even for kingship over the three worlds, much less for the earth.

In slaying the sons of Dhṛitarāshṭra what delight would be ours, O Janārdana? Evil would but overtake us, if we slew those desperadoes.

Hence it is not fitting for us to slay the sons of Dhṛitarāshṭra our kinsfolk. For if we slay our kin, how should we be happy, O Mādhava?

Even if they, with hearts overcome by greed, see no wrong in destroying a family, or crime in wronging friends,

How should we not know how to turn away from that sin, who see the wrong of destroying a family, O Janārdana?

40. When a family is destroyed, the eternal family laws of righteousness perish; when the righteousness is destroyed, unrighteousness overcomes the whole family.

When unrighteousness prevails, O Kṛishṇa,

the women of the family are corrupted; when the women are corrupted, O son of Vṛishṇi, there arises confusion of caste.

The confusion results in hell for the slayers of families and the family; the fathers[1] fall, for they are deprived of the balls of rice and water offered to the dead.

Through these sins of the slayers of families, these sins that cause confusion of caste, the eternal laws of righteousness both of birth and family are ruined.

The abode ordained for men whose family laws of righteousness are ruined, O Janārdana, is ever in hell. Thus we have heard.

45. Oh, alas! a great sin we have undertaken to commit, in that out of greed for the pleasures of kingship we are seeking to slay our own people.

If the sons of Dhṛitarāshṭra with weapons in hand should slay me unresisting and weaponless in the battle, that were better for me.

Sanjaya said: Thus Arjuna spoke on the battle-field, and sank down on the chariot-seat. He dropped his bow and arrows, his mind shaken with grief.

[1] The deceased ancestors, to whom sacrifices for their welfare are due.

II

SĀNKHYA

Kṛishṇa tells Arjuna that he is mistaken in grieving, for the soul never dies. He ought to fight without the wish for personal gain. This is the Sānkhya teaching. Kṛishṇa then shows him the advantages of Yoga, in which by training his intellect he can become free from the power of the senses and attain peace.

SANJAYA said: To Arjuna, full of pity and despondent, his eyes dimmed with overflowing tears, Madhusūdana spoke thus:

The Lord said: Whence in this strait has come upon thee this baseness, not practised by the noble, not leading to heaven, not bringing honour, O Arjuna?

Yield not to unmanliness, O son of Pṛithā: that befits thee not. Abandon base weakness of heart, and stand up, O hero.

Arjuna said: How shall I fight in battle with arrows against Bhīshma and Droṇa, O Madhusūdana, who are worthy of reverence, O Arisūdana?

5. For rather than slay those teachers of great power it is better even to eat the food of beggars here in the world; but if I were to slay those teachers here, who desire my good, I should enjoy pleasures besmeared with blood.

Nor do we know which would be better, for

us to conquer them or for them to conquer us, and if we should slay them we should not wish to live, even the sons of Dhṛitarāshṭra arrayed before us.

My nature is overcome with the fault of meanness; my thought of duty is confused. I ask thee which would be the better; tell me with certainty. I am thy disciple, teach me, who have come to thee.

For I see not what would drive away the sorrow that dries up my senses, if I should attain prosperous kingship on earth without a rival, or even sovereignty among the gods.

Sanjaya said: Thus Guḍākeśa the hero addressed Hṛishīkeśa, and saying to Govinda, "I will not fight," became silent.

10. Then Hṛishīkeśa, as though smiling, between the two armies said to the despondent one.

The Lord said: Thou hast sorrowed for whom thou shouldst not sorrow, and yet utterest wise things.[1] Neither for the dead nor the living do sages grieve.

Never at any time was I not, nor thou, nor these lords of men, nor shall any of us ever cease to be hereafter.

[1] According to Ānandagiri this refers to Arjuna's words in I, 43, about the sin of destroying families. The Kashmir recension has, "thou dost not speak as an intelligent man"; but this, as Dr. Barnett points out, may be an emendation to remove a supposed contradiction.

As in this body the dweller therein passes through childhood, youth, and age, so he attains to another body. The steadfast man is not confused thereat.

But contacts with the things of sense, O son of Kuntī, which cause cold and heat, pleasure and pain, come and go without permanence. Endure them, O Bhārata.

15. For indeed the man whom they distress not, O chief of men, facing equally pain and pleasure, and steadfast, is fit for immortality.

The unreal has no existence, the real is never non-existent; the conclusion about both these has been perceived by the seers of the truth.

But know that indestructible is this (ātman), by which this all has been created[1]; no one can work the destruction of this changeless one.

Finite are called the bodies of the eternal embodied one, which is indestructible and immeasurable. Therefore fight, O Bhārata.

He that regards it as a slayer, and he that thinks it is slain, both of them understand not. It slays not, nor is it slain.

20. It is born not, nor does it ever die, nor shall it, after having been brought into being, come not to be hereafter. The unborn, the permanent, the

[1] *Tatam*, the word means "stretched on a loom, woven," and is due to the Vedic conception of the universe as the warp and woof of a loom. Śaṅkara, followed by modern commentators, says *vyāptam*, "enveloped."

eternal, the ancient, it is slain not when the body is slain.

He that knows it to be indestructible, permanent, unborn, and changeless, how can that man, O son of Pṛithā, and whom, can he cause to be slain or slay?

As a man casting off his worn-out clothes takes other new ones, so the embodied one, casting off its worn-out bodies, enters others that are new.

Weapons cleave it not, fire burns it not, water wets it not, nor do the winds dry it.

Uncleavable is it, it cannot be burnt, it cannot be wetted or dried; permanent, all-pervading, stable is it, immovable and eternal.

25. Unmanifested, inconceivable, unchanging it is called. Therefore knowing it to be such thou shouldst not sorrow.

If thou thinkest of it as continually born, and continually dying, even so, O mighty-armed, thou shouldst not sorrow.

For him that is born death is certain, and certain is birth for him that is dead. Therefore when a thing is unavoidable, thou shouldst not sorrow.

Unmanifest are creatures in their beginning, manifest in their middle state, so are they unmanifest in their ending. What room for lamentation is there herein?

As marvellous one man looks upon it, likewise

as marvellous another speaks of it, and as marvellous another hears of it. But not one even when he has heard of it knows it.

30. This embodied one in the body of everyone is ever invulnerable, O Bhārata. Therefore for no creature shouldst thou sorrow.

And so, looking to thy own duty, thou shouldst not tremble; for there is nought better to a warrior than righteous war.

Happy are the warriors, O son of Pṛithā, who obtain such a fight offered freely to them as the open door of heaven.

So if thou wilt not undertake this righteous warfare, then thou wilt cast away thy own duty and honour, and fall into sin.

And people will speak of thy undying dishonour; and to an honourable man dishonour is worse than death.

35. The men of the great chariots will think that thou hast held back from battle through fear; and thou who wast highly esteemed by them wilt be lightly thought of.

Many words that should not be said will thy enemies speak, blaming thy prowess. What is more painful than that?

If slain, thou wilt attain heaven, or if thou dost conquer, thou wilt enjoy the earth. Therefore arise, O son of Kuntī, and be resolved on action.

Hold pleasure and pain equal, gain and loss,

victory and defeat ; and therefore gird thyself for the fight. So shalt thou not fall into sin.

The thought[1] here (set forth) has been declared to thee according to Sānkhya. But now hear it according to Yoga. Trained by this thought, O son of Pṛithā, thou shalt cast off the bond of action.

40. There is here no failure in the undertaking, no obstacle. Even a little of this righteousness saves from great fear.

This thought, which is of constant nature, O son of Kuru, is one. But many-branched and endless are the thoughts of the inconstant.

Through that flowery speech which the unwise proclaim, delighting in the word of the Vedas, O son of Pṛithā, and saying there is nought but this,

Whose souls are full of desire, intent on heaven, —through that speech which offers birth as the fruit of action, which contains many various rites for attaining enjoyments and lordship,

Through that speech of those who cling to enjoyments and lordship, and whose minds are carried away, this constant thought is not produced in concentration.

45. The Vedas have the three constituents as

[1] The word here translated "thought" is *buddhi*. It is the teaching concerning action which has just been given. Later, when the word is used in a technical sense as one of the evolutes of Nature, and as the mental function to be trained by Yoga, it is translated "intellect."

their objects.[1] Become free from the three constituents, O Arjuna, free from the pairs of opposites, abiding ever in goodness free from the keeping of possessions, possessing the self.

As many as are the uses of a tank, whose waters flow in from all sides, so many are the uses of all the Vedas for a brahmin who understands.[2]

Thy business should be with action, never with the fruits; let not thy motive be the fruit of action, nor be attached to non-action.

Abiding in Yoga perform actions and abandon attachment, O Dhananjaya, evenly balanced in success or failure. Yoga is called evenness (equanimity).

For lower by far is action [3] than the Yoga of the intellect, O Dhananjaya. Seek refuge in the intellect. Wretched are they whose motive is the fruit of works.

50. He who is trained in intellect abandons both

[1] For the constituents, see p. 19; the Vedas deal with the objects of the world of sense, ritual and sacrifice, not with the means of winning final release. The pairs of opposites are pleasure and pain, desire and aversion, etc.

[2] Meaning that the Vedas may have many uses for one who knows how to apply them, though not for attaining the highest end; but it has also been taken in the sense that where there is much water a tank is of no use at all.

[3] This, as Śankara says, and as the last words of the verse show, is ordinary action done for the sake of the fruit; the Yoga is the training of the intellect so as to act without desire for the fruit.

good and evil deeds. Therefore train thyself in Yoga. Yoga is skill in actions.

For the wise who are trained in intellect renounce the fruit produced by action; they are released from the bonds of birth, and go to the abode free from sickness.

When thy intellect shall pass beyond the tangle of bewilderment, then wilt thou reach indifference about what is to be heard or has been heard.

When thy intellect, bewildered by what has been heard, shall stand steady, unmoving in concentration, then shalt thou attain to Yoga.

Arjuna said: What is the description of him whose knowledge is fixed, and who is fixed in concentration? How will one speak whose thought is fixed, and how will he sit or move?

55. The Lord said: When he abandons all desires of the mind, O son of Pṛithā, and is satisfied in the self by the self, he is called one whose knowledge is fixed.

He whose mind is not agitated amid pains, who amid pleasures has no longings, and from whom passion, fear, and anger have departed, is called a recluse whose thought is fixed.

He who is without affection on all sides, whatever good or bad fortune is his lot, and who is neither glad nor hates—the knowledge of that man is fixed.

And when, like a tortoise withdrawing its limbs on every side, he withdraws his senses from the objects of sense, his knowledge is fixed.

Objects of sense turn away from an embodied one who is abstinent; to abandoning of taste turns the taste of one who has seen the highest.

60. Yet the harassing senses, O son of Kuntī, even of a wise man who is striving, carry away his mind violently.

Let him restrain them all, and trained let him sit intent on me; for when his senses are under control, his knowledge is fixed.

If a man meditates on the objects of sense, attachment to them arises; from attachment desire is born; from desire anger is produced.

Through anger comes bewilderment, through bewilderment wandering of memory, through confusion of memory destruction of the intellect, through destruction of the intellect he is destroyed.

But he who with obedient self goes among the objects of sense with his senses detached from passion and aversion, and under the control of the self, attains to serenity.

65. In serenity the disappearance of his pains is produced; for the intellect of him whose mind is serene quickly becomes fixed.

There is no intellect for the untrained, nor for the untrained is there the practice of meditation, nor for him who does not meditate is there peace; for him without peace much less is there happiness.

For whichever of the roving senses the mind obeys, that carries away his knowledge, as wind drives a ship on the waters.

Therefore, O mighty-armed one, when the senses of a man are withheld from the objects of sense, his knowledge is fixed.

In that which is night for all creatures he who is restrained is awake; in that in which all creatures are awake, that is night for the recluse who sees.

70. As waters enter the ocean, which is filled yet immovably fixed, even so he into whom all desires flow attains to peace, not he that desires desires.

The man who forsakes all desires, and moves without longing, without the thought of mine, or I, attains to peace.

This is the Brahma-state, O son of Pṛithā. He who at the hour of death abides in it gains the nirvāṇa of Brahma.

III

ACTION

Arjuna asks why, if Yoga is best, he must act. The Lord shows that in any case action is inevitable. Actions themselves are a training (Yoga) by which to become free from the passions. He should recognise that the constituents (the forces of nature and the passions of the mind) interact not with the soul but among themselves. He must thus keep out of the power of the passions by not being attached to actions.

ARJUNA said: If intellect is deemed by thee to be more excellent than action, O Janārdana, why dost thou impose upon me a terrible action, O Keśava?

With this perplexing speech thou somehow bewilderest my intellect. Tell me therefore clearly the one thing whereby I may attain the better course.

The Lord said: In this world there is a twofold position, which I have told before, O sinless one: that of the Sānkhyas through the Yoga of knowledge, and that of the Yogis through the Yoga of action.

Not by refusing to undertake action does a man enjoy non-action, nor by mere renunciation does he win success.

5. For no one ever, even for a moment, remains without doing action; everyone is made to do action through the constituents of Nature.

He who controls his organs of action, and sits reflecting in his mind on the objects of the senses, bewildered in soul, is called one of false conduct.

But he who restrains his senses by his mind, and undertakes the Yoga of action by means of the organs of action, being unattached, excels.

Do thou prescribed action. Action is more excellent than non-action. Even the maintenance of thy body would not be achieved if thou didst not act.

Except for the action done for the sake of sacrifice, this world is bound by action. For the sake of that, O son of Kuntī, do thou action, free from attachment.

10. Prajāpati[1] aforetime created beings along with sacrifice, and said, "By this ye shall propagate. Be this to you the cow of desires.[2]

With this nourish ye the gods. May the gods nourish you. If ye nourish one another, ye will the better attain the Supreme.

For the gods, nourished by sacrifice, shall grant you your wished-for enjoyments. He who enjoys, and does not offer to them what they have given, is a thief."

[1] The creator in Vedic mythology.

[2] A mythical cow of Indra, from which everything desired could be had; see X, 27.

The good, who eat the remains of the sacrifice, are freed from all faults; but the wicked, who cook for their own sakes, eat sin.

From food beings arise; from rain food is produced; from the sacrifice arises rain; the sacrifice is produced by action.

15. Know that action is produced from Brahma[1]; Brahma is produced from the imperishable. Therefore Brahma all-pervading is ever-present in the sacrifice.

So he who in this world turns not the wheel that has been set revolving, evil of life and delighting in the senses, lives in vain, O son of Pṛithā.

But the man who rejoices in the self, who is satisfied in the self, and who is content in the self, for him there is nought remaining to be done.

For him in this world there is no purpose in what is done, nor any in what is not done, nor is there dependence of his purpose on any being.

Therefore without attachment ever perform action that should be done; for by doing action without attachment a man attains the Supreme.

[1] Here in the Vedic sense of prayer or magical formula, especially the mantras of the Vedas used in the sacrifice; cf. *Vedic Hymns*, pp. 21, 125. In IV, 24, where it is explained that any action may be a sacrifice, Brahma is the Supreme. For Brahmā the god, see note on VIII, 3.

20. Verily by action Janaka[1] and others attained success; so too, looking to the welfare of the world, shouldst thou do action.

Whatever an eminent man performs, so do other men act; the standard that he sets up people follow.

There is nought to be done by me in the three worlds, O son of Pṛithā, nor aught to be attained that is attainable. Yet I engage in action.

For if I did not engage in action unwearied, (though) it is my path that they follow from all directions,

These worlds would fall into ruin, if I did not perform action, and I should be the maker of confusion, and should destroy these creatures.

25. As the ignorant act with attachment to action, O Bhārata, so let the wise man act without attachment, desirous of benefiting the world.

Let not the wise man, who is trained in conduct, cause distraction of intellect in the ignorant who are attached to action. Let him cause them to delight in all actions.

Actions are done wholly by the constituents of Nature. The soul that is bewildered by the thought of I thinks, "I am the actor."

But he who knows the truth, O mighty-armed, concerning the parts played by the

[1] King of Mithilā and father of Sītā, the wife of Rāma.

constituents and actions, thinking, "the constituents move among the constituents," is not attached.

Those who are bewildered by the constituents of Nature are those attached to the actions of the constituents. Let not him whose knowledge is complete mislead the dull of imperfect knowledge.

30. Resigning all actions to me, with thy thought on that present in the self, do thou without hope, and without the thought of mine, fight freed from thy fever.

They also, who ever follow my teaching, full of faith and without ill-will, are released from actions.

But they who are ill-willed towards my teaching and follow it not, know thou that they, mindless ones, are bewildered in all knowledge and are destroyed.

The man of knowledge too is active in accordance with his own Nature. Beings follow Nature. What can restraint do ?

Passion and aversion lie in the objects of each sense. Let no one come into the power of those two, for they obstruct him in the way.

35. Better is one's own duty without merit than the duty of another well performed. Better is death in performing one's own duty. Another's duty brings danger.

Arjuna said: Then by what is the man urged

on that he commits sin, even without wishing it, as though constrained by force, O descendant of Vṛishṇi ?

The Lord said : It is desire, it is anger, produced by the constituent of passion, the voracious one, the wicked. Know that in this world that is the enemy.

As a flame enveloped in smoke, as a mirror by dirt, as an embryo by its covering, so is this world enveloped by that.

Enveloped is the knowledge of the knower by this constant enemy, which takes what form it wills, O son of Kuntī, and is an insatiable flame.

40. The senses, the mind, and the intellect are said to be its basis ; with these it bewilders the embodied one, enveloping his knowledge.

Therefore first restraining the senses, O best of Bharatas, do thou slay this wicked one that destroys knowledge and understanding.

They say that the senses are high ; higher than the senses is the mind, higher than the mind the intellect, but higher than the intellect is He.

Thus understanding what is higher than the intellect, and establishing the self by the self, O mighty-armed, slay the enemy, which takes what form it wills, and is hard to approach.

IV

KNOWLEDGE

By the practice of Yoga knowledge is attained, not merely (as in the Sānkhya and Yoga philosophies) the knowledge that the soul is distinct from Nature, nor even, as in Vedānta, the knowledge that all is one, but the knowledge that this One is the Lord, who wishes all to come to him and shows them the way. With this knowledge every action dedicated to God is a sacrifice.

THE Lord said: To Vivasvant I proclaimed this changeless Yoga, Vivasvant declared it to Manu, Manu told it to Ikshvāku.[1]

So receiving it in succession the royal sages knew it. Here in the world through the lapse of long time this Yoga has been destroyed, O hero.

Even this ancient Yoga has to-day been declared by me to thee. Thou art my devoted one and friend; for this is the supreme secret.

Arjuna said: Thy birth was after, the birth of Vivasvant was before. How am I to understand this, that thou didst proclaim it in the beginning?

5. The Lord said: Many births have I left behind, and many hast thou, O Arjuna. I know them all, but thou knowest them not, O hero.

[1] These are ancestors in the solar line of kings. Vivasvant is the sun himself.

Though I am the unborn, the unchanging self, though Lord of creatures, I condition my own Nature, and am born by my magic power.[1]

For whenever there is a decay of righteousness, O Bhārata, and a rising of unrighteousness, then I emit myself.

In order to save the good, and to destroy evil-doers, to establish righteousness I am born from age to age.[2]

He who knows in truth my divine birth and action when he abandons a body goes not to birth again; he goes to me, O Arjuna.

10. Many there are who, freed from passion, fear, and anger, becoming one with me, depending on me, and purified with the austerity of knowledge, have entered into my being.

In the way that men approach me, even so do I impart myself to them; it is my path that they follow from all directions.

They that desire the success of their actions in this world sacrifice to the gods; for quickly in the world of men comes success born of action.

The four castes were emitted by me according

[1] *Māyā*, see Introd., p. 15.

[2] Nine incarnations are spoken of and one to come, but there are many more. Śrī Gaurānga (Chaitanya), who appeared as a religious reformer in Bengal in the fifteenth century, is held by the Vaishnavas of Bengal to be "neither a human personality, nor even an incarnation, but the absolute Being Bhagavān himself."—G. B. Mallik, *The Philosophy of the Vaiṣṇava Religion*, vol. i, p. 234.

to the distribution of the constituents (of Nature) and actions. Know me, though without action and changeless, as the doer thereof.

Actions stain me not; no desire have I for the fruit of actions. He who thus understands me is not bound by actions.

15. With this knowledge action was done also by men of old who desired release. Therefore so do thou do action as was done before by men of old.

What is action, what is non-action? Herein even sages have been perplexed. What that action is I will tell thee, by knowing which thou mayest be released from evil.

For what action is one should learn, and one should learn what is wrong action; and what is non-action one should learn. Impenetrable is the course of action.

He who sees non-action in action, and action in non-action, that man has intelligence among men; he who is trained is a doer of every action.

He whose every undertaking is without desire or purpose, and whose work is burnt up with the fire of knowledge, is called learned by the wise.

20. When he has abandoned attachment to the fruit of actions, ever contented and without support, even though he is occupied in action, he performs none.

Without hope, with his mind and self restrained,

abandoning all possessions, doing merely that action required by the body, he acquires no guilt.

Satisfied with what he gets by chance, he has passed beyond the pairs; he is unenvious, even-minded in success or failure, so that although he acts he is not bound.

When one has become free from attachment, has won release, and has his mind established in knowledge, performing sacrifice, all his action is annihilated.

The act of offering is Brahma, the oblation is Brahma, it is Brahma that is offered by Brahma in the fire; by that to Brahma must he come through concentration on action which is Brahma.[1]

25. Some Yogis worship with a sacrifice to the gods. Others celebrate a sacrifice only by sacrifice to Brahma as the fire.

Others sacrifice their hearing and other senses in the fires of restraint. Others sacrifice sound and other objects of sense in the fires of the senses.

And others sacrifice all the actions of the senses and the actions of breath in the fire of Yoga and the restraining of the self, lit by knowledge.

Others are sacrificers of wealth, sacrificers of austerity, and sacrificers of Yoga; men of restraint and of strict vows are sacrificers of their scripture-study and knowledge.

[1] See note on III, 15.

Others sacrifice their outbreathing in their inbreathing, and their inbreathing in their outbreathing. They check the breath that goes in and out, intent on control of breathing.

30. Others restrained in food offer breaths in breaths. All these too are knowers of sacrifice, whose sins are done away by sacrifice.

Eaters of the immortal food of the remains of the sacrifice, they go to Brahma the eternal. This world is not for him who sacrifices not, much less another world, O best of Kurus.

Even thus, many and various are the sacrifices that are set up before Brahma. Know that they are all born of action, and thus knowing thou shalt be liberated.

Better than material sacrifice is the sacrifice of knowledge, O hero. Each and every action, O son of Pṛithā, is comprehended in knowledge.

Learn this by doing obeisance, by putting questions, by serving ; the seers of the truth, who have knowledge, will teach thee knowledge.

35. When thou knowest this, thou wilt not again fall into bewilderment, O son of Pāṇḍu. Through this thou shalt behold all beings in the self, and thus in me.

Even though thou art the chief sinner of all sinners, it is by the raft of knowledge that thou shalt cross over all wickedness.

As a burning fire reduces its fuel to ashes, O

Arjuna, so the fire of knowledge reduces all actions to ashes.

For no purifier can be found in the world like knowledge. He who has attained to Yoga, himself finds it in time in the self.

The man of faith gains knowledge, intent on it with senses restrained ; when he has gained it, in no long time he attains to supreme peace.

40. But the man who is ignorant and without faith, and who doubts, is destroyed ; there is neither this world nor another nor happiness for him who doubts.

He who through Yoga has renounced action, whose doubt has been cloven asunder by knowledge, who possesses the self, is not bound by actions, O Dhananjaya.

Therefore with the self's sword of knowledge cleave asunder the doubt born of ignorance, which abides in thy heart. Be established in Yoga and stand up, O Bhārata.

V

RENUNCIATION OF ACTIONS

Actions may be renounced, as by the ascetic, who deliberately refrains from certain actions,[1] or they may be performed without attachment and with abandonment of the fruit. The latter is called the Yoga of action, and is the better, but without the method of Yoga-practice is hard to attain. The Lord gives further instruction on this practice.

ARJUNA said: Thou praisest the renunciation of actions, O Kṛishṇa, and also the Yoga (of actions). Of these two which is the better? Tell me with certainty.

The Lord said: Renunciation (of actions) and the Yoga of actions both lead to the highest state; but of these the Yoga of actions is superior to the renunciation of actions.

He is to be known as a perpetual renouncer who neither hates nor wishes; for one who is without the pairs, O mighty-armed, is easily freed from bondage.

They are fools, not learned, who declare Sānkhya and Yoga to be different; he who is established only in one gains the fruit of both.

5. The place that is obtained by the Sānkhyas is reached also by the practisers of Yoga.

[1] There are some actions that ought not to be renounced, as is explained in XVIII.

He who sees that Sānkhya and Yoga are one he sees.

But renunciation, O mighty-armed, is hard to obtain without Yoga. The recluse trained in Yoga in no long time reaches Brahma.

He who is trained in Yoga, with the self purified, the self subdued, and the senses overcome, and whose self has become the self of all beings, even though he act is not stained.

He who is trained, a knower of the truth, should think, "I do not do anything," whether seeing, hearing, touching, smelling, eating, walking, sleeping, or breathing,

Whether speaking, letting go or grasping, or opening and closing the eyes, still remembering that the senses move among the objects of the senses.

10. He who places his actions on Brahma, who abandons attachment, and thus acts, is not stained by sin, like a lotus leaf unstained by water.

It is only through the body, the mind, the intellect, and the senses that Yogis perform action, abandoning attachment for the purification of the self.

He who is trained, abandoning the fruit of works, attains to final peace. He who is untrained, acting through desire, and attached to the fruit, is bound.

With his mind renouncing all actions, the

embodied one sits happily in control in the nine-gated city (the body), neither acting nor causing to act.

This Lord (the self) produces neither agency nor actions of the world, nor the union of action and fruit, but it is nature which accomplishes.

15. The Lord takes neither the sin of anyone nor the good deed. Knowledge is enveloped by ignorance; through this are creatures bewildered.

But for those whose ignorance of the self through knowledge is destroyed, their knowledge, like the sun, illumines the Supreme.

Having their intellect on that (Supreme), their self on that, their resolution on that, their object that, they go to the place from where there is no return, their sins removed by knowledge.

A brahmin endowed with knowledge and discipline, a cow, an elephant, even a dog and a cooker of dogs, are looked upon by the learned as equal.

Even in this world rebirth is overcome by those whose mind stays in equanimity; for Brahma is without fault and equal; therefore they stay in Brahma.

20. One will not be elated at gaining something pleasant, nor agitated at gaining something unpleasant; he is firm of intellect, un-

bewildered, the knower of Brahma, staying in Brahma.

In that he whose self is unattached to outer contacts finds happiness in the self, he with his self trained by the Yoga of Brahma enjoys imperishable happiness.

For enjoyments born of contact have their origin in pain; they have beginning and end, O son of Kuntī. The wise man does not rejoice in them.

He who in this world before being released from the body is able to endure the agitation arising from desire and anger, he is trained, he is a happy man.

He who is happy within, who rejoices within, who also has light within, he, a Yogi, becomes Brahma, and attains to the nirvāṇa of Brahma.

25. Sages, whose sins are destroyed, their doubts split, their selves restrained, rejoicing in the welfare of all beings, win the nirvāṇa of Brahma.

To those who are detached from desire and anger, who practise restraint, who are restrained in mind, and who know the self, the nirvāṇa of Brahma is near.

When he has put external contacts outside, has placed his gaze between his eyebrows, and has made his outbreathing and his inbreathing equal, as they move between the nostrils,

The recluse, restrained in senses, mind, and

intellect, intent on release, freed from desire, fear, and anger, in truth he is ever released.

When he knows me as the enjoyer of sacrifice and austerity, as the great Lord of all the worlds and the friend of all beings, he attains to peace.

VI

MEDITATION

Continuation of instruction on Yoga and eulogy of the practice.

THE Lord said: He who, without dependence on the fruit of action, does the action that he ought, is one who has renounced; he is a Yogi, not he who is without fire and ceremonies.

What they call renunciation, know that it is Yoga, O son of Pāṇḍu. For no one who has not renounced purpose [1] becomes a Yogi.

The mark of the recluse who is wishing to reach the summit of Yoga is called action; but the mark of him who has reached the summit of Yoga is called tranquillity.

For when he who has renounced all purposes is

[1] The purpose of acting so as to gain the fruit.

not attached to objects of sense or to actions, he is said to have reached the summit of Yoga.

5. Let him raise the self by the self, let him not depress the self; for the self is indeed the friend of the self; the self is indeed the self's enemy.

The self is a friend of the self of him by whom the self is conquered by the self. But the self should behave as an enemy in enmity with the non-self (individuality as opposed to the higher self).

The higher[1] self of one whose (lower) self is conquered and appeased is concentrated, whether he is in cold or heat, pleasure or pain, in honour or dishonour.

The Yogi, to whom a clod, a stone, and gold are the same, is called one whose self is contented with knowledge and understanding, who stands unshakable, with senses subdued, and who is trained.

He whose intellect is the same amid lovers, friends, enemies, the indifferent, neutrals, opponents, and relatives, amid good and bad, excels.

10. A Yogi should constantly train his self, staying in a secret place, alone, controlling his mind, free from hope and possessions.

In a pure place, setting up for himself a firm

[1] This gives the required meaning, but *paramātman* usually means the supreme self.

seat, not too high, not too low, with cloth, antelope skin, and kuśa grass upon it,

There bringing his mind to one point, restraining the action of the mind and senses, and sitting on the seat, he should practise Yoga for the purifying of the self.

Holding his body, head, and neck evenly, firm without motion, looking at the point of his nose, and not looking round about him.

With his self at peace, freed from fear, abiding in the vow of celibacy, restraining his mind, trained with his thought on me, let him sit intent on me.

15. Thus ever training his self, the Yogi with mind restrained attains to peace, to the highest nirvāṇa, which exists in me.

Yoga is not for one who eats too much, nor for one who fasts excessively, nor for one of very sleepy habit, nor for the sleepless, O Arjuna.

For him who is trained in food and recreation, whose activities are trained in performing actions, who is trained in sleeping and in waking, Yoga becomes a destroyer of pain.

When his mind is restrained and fixed on the self, without longing for any desires, then he is called trained.

As a lamp in a windless place flickers not, so is this deemed to be a likeness of the Yogi of restrained mind, who practises Yoga of the self.

20. (This practice) wherein the mind finds rest, stopped by the exercise of Yoga, and where, seeing the self by the self, he is satisfied in the self,

This immeasurable happiness which he knows, to be grasped only by the intellect and beyond the senses, wherein he stays and moves not from the real,

And which, when he has gained he thinks there is no gain beyond it, and abiding in which he is not shaken even by heavy pain,

This separation from conjunction with pain should be known as Yoga. This Yoga should be practised with resolution and undesponding mind.

Abandoning entirely all the desires that arise from purpose, curbing with his mind the multitude of the senses all round,

25. Little by little let him come to rest with his intellect held by firmness, and making his mind stay in the self, let him not think of anything.

Whenever the mind, wavering and unfixed, goes out, let him restrain it and bring it under the control of the self.

For the highest happiness comes upon the Yogi whose mind is calmed, in whom passion is appeased, who has become Brahma and free from sin.

The Yogi ever training his self, with his sins

gone, easily enjoys the infinite happiness of contact with Brahma.

He whose self is trained by Yoga, with even gaze everywhere beholds his self abiding in all beings and all beings in his self.

30. When one sees me everywhere, and sees everything in me, I am never lost to him nor is he lost to me.

He who resorts to me as abiding in all beings, who is established in oneness, however he spends his life, he as a Yogi dwells in me.

He who through likeness to the self sees equality everywhere, O Arjuna, whether pleasant or painful, he is deemed a supreme Yogi.

Arjuna said: Because of unsteadiness, O Madhusūdana, I do not see the firm continuance of this Yoga, which thou hast declared to be through equanimity.

For the mind is unsteady, O Kṛishṇa, harassing, violent, and obstinate. To curb it I think is as hard as to curb the wind.

35. The Lord said: Doubtless, O mighty-armed, the mind is hard to curb and restless; but by exercise, O son of Kuntī, and absence of passion it is captured.

By one whose self is unrestrained Yoga is hard to win, I hold; but one whose self is controlled and who is restrained can win it by the right means.

Arjuna said: The unrestrained who is endowed

with faith, but whose mind wanders from Yoga, and who does not attain success in Yoga, what way does he go, O Kṛishṇa ?

Is he then fallen from both, and destroyed like a scattered cloud, not being established, O mighty-armed, but bewildered on the path of Brahma ?

Deign, O Kṛishṇa, to dispel this my doubt utterly ; for there is no other dispeller of this doubt save thee.

40. The Lord said : O son of Pṛithā, neither here nor in the next world is there destruction for him ; for no one, my son, who does good goes an evil way.

After reaching the worlds of the doers of merit and dwelling there for numberless years, he who has fallen from Yoga is born in a house of the pure and prosperous.

Or he is reborn even in a family of wise Yogis ; yet such a birth as that in the world is harder to win.

There he acquires the contact with intellect which he had in his former body, and from there he strives further for success, O child of Kuru.

For by that very former exercise he is carried on, even without his will ; and also desiring to know Yoga he passes beyond the Brahma (manifested) in the word.

45. But the Yogi who strives with great striving, purified from sin, after successfully passing

through many births thereafter goes the highest way.

Higher than ascetics is the Yogi, higher too than men of knowledge is he held; higher than performers of action is the Yogi. Therefore become a Yogi, O Arjuna.

But even of all Yogis he who with his inner self has gone to me, who worships me with faith, he, I hold, is the best trained.

VII

KNOWLEDGE OF THE LORD

The Lord begins the exposition of his being as comprising all manifested things in his lower nature, but as being in his higher nature the reality behind them, and shows how it is hard to reach the reality.

HEAR how, when thy mind is attached to me, O son of Pṛithā, and when thou practisest Yoga with me as thy resort, thou mayest without doubt know me entirely.

I will declare to thee fully the knowledge and understanding, which when thou knowest nought else here remains to be known.

Among thousands of human beings, but some

individual strives for success. Even of the strivers who have been successful but some individual knows me in reality.

Earth, water, fire, air, space, mind, intellect, and the thought of I (individuality), these form my nature in its eightfold division.[1]

5. This is my lower nature. But know that other than this is my higher nature. It is the life-principle, O mighty-armed, by which the world is sustained.

Understand that therefrom all beings have their source ; I am the origin and likewise the dissolution of the whole world.

There is nothing higher than I, O Dhananjaya ; on me all this is strung like jewels on a thread.

I am taste in water, O son of Kuntī, I am splendour in the moon and sun, I am the sacred syllable in all the Vedas, sound in space, and maleness in men.

I am pure smell in earth, brilliance in fire, life in all beings, and austerity in the austere.

10. Know that I am the eternal seed of all beings, O son of Pṛithā, the intellect of the intelligent, the brilliance of the brilliant.

I am the strength of the strong, free from desire

[1] These are the forms which unmanifested Nature takes when it becomes manifested. They appear to be an early classification, which was elaborated into twenty-four. A longer list is given in XIII, 5, which almost coincides with that of classical Sānkhya.

and passion. Desire not forbidden by duty am I among beings, O best of Bharatas.

And know that natures that are of the constituents of goodness, passion, and dullness[1] are from me, but I am not in them, they are in me.

By these natures formed of the three constituents the whole world is bewildered; it knows not me the supreme above them and changeless.

For this my divine delusion (māyā), due to the constituents, is hard to pass. Only they who resort to me pass beyond this delusion.

15. Evildoers, bewildered, the lowest of men, resort not to me. With their knowledge carried away by delusion they have betaken themselves to an ungodly nature.

Four kinds of people worship me, they who act well, O Arjuna, the afflicted one, the one eager to know, the one who wants the useful,[2] and the man of knowledge, O best of Bharatas.

Of these the man of knowledge, perpetually trained, devoted to one only, is pre-eminent; for I am dear beyond anything to the man of knowledge, and he is dear to me.

[1] In material natures these appear as lightness, motion, and heaviness.

[2] Śankara interprets as *dhanakāmo*, "desirous of wealth." There are here four stages of people, one who has suffered losses, one who desires something better, one who wants something good but does not necessarily know what it is, and one who does know.

Eminent indeed are all these, but the man of knowledge I deem to be myself; for he with his self trained is established in me, the highest way.

At the end of many births the man of knowledge resorts to me, saying, "Vāsudeva is all"; a man of great soul is hard to find.

20. Those whose knowledge is carried away by various desires resort to other divinities; having recourse to various rules of restraint they are restrained by their own Nature.

If any devout one wishes with faith to worship any form, it is I who impart to him that steady faith.

Trained by this faith he tries to propitiate it, and thence receives his desires; for it is by me that they are bestowed.

But the fruit of these men of little sense has an end. To the gods they go who sacrifice to gods, but those devoted to me go to me.

Those without intellect think of me the unmanifested as manifestation, not knowing my highest nature, the changeless, the supreme.

25. I am not evident to everyone, being enveloped by the delusion of my Yoga.[1] This bewildered world knows me not as the unborn, the changeless.

I know the beings of the past and the present, O

[1] Kṛishṇa is the Lord of Yoga, and through the powers such as even the ordinary Yogi may acquire can delude.

Arjuna, and those of the future; but no one knows me.

Through the bewilderment of the pairs, which arises from desire and hate, O Bhārata, all beings fall into bewilderment in being born, O hero.

But they in whom sin has ceased, and who act virtuously, released from the bewilderment of the pairs and firm in their vows, worship me.

They who strive for release from old age and death, depending on me, know Brahma complete as present in the self, and all action.

30. And they who know me as present in beings, as present in the gods, and as present in the sacrifice, they also at the time of their departure know me with trained minds.

VIII

THE LORD AS BRAHMA THE IMPERISHABLE

The Lord explains certain terms used in the previous chapter, and tells how the Yogi at death may escape rebirth. At the time of his death he must think on Kṛishṇa as Brahma, and must die at a certain auspicious time.

ARJUNA said: What is that Brahma, what is that present in the self, what is action, O highest Person ? What is that which has been declared as present in beings, and what is that which is called the present in the gods ?

How and who is it that is the present in the sacrifice, here in the body, O Madhusūdana ? And how at the time of departure art thou to be known by those in whom the self is trained ?

The Lord said : Brahma [1] is the indestructible, the supreme ; its nature is called the present in the self. The emission (creation) that causes the birth of beings is called action.

The present in beings is perishable nature ; the present in the gods is the Person [2] ; I am the present in the sacrifice here in the body, O best of embodied ones.

5. He who at the time of death, when released from the body, goes forth thinking on me, goes to my nature ; of that there is no doubt.

Or on whatever being one thinks, when at death he abandons his body, to that being he goes, O son of Kuntī, ever conformed to that being.

Therefore at all times think upon me and fight. With thy mind and intellect dedicated to me thou shalt come to me, there is no doubt.

With his mind trained by the Yoga of exercise, not going elsewhere, one goes to the supreme

[1] Brahma as the one reality is neuter. Brahmā (masculine) is a god, and like the other gods only one manifestation of Kṛishṇa or the real, as in XI, 15.

[2] *Purusha ;* this is the usual term in Sānkhya for the self.

Person, the divine, if he thinks upon him, O son of Pṛithā.

He who thinks upon the Seer, the Instructor, the more minute than the minute, the Disposer of all, of inconceivable form, bright as the sun, beyond the darkness,

10. Then at the time of his departure, that man with unshaken mind, trained by devotion and the power of Yoga, making his breath duly pass between his eyebrows, goes to the supreme Person, the divine.

That which the knowers of the Vedas call the indestructible, into which the restrained, free from passion enter, and through desire for which they practise celibacy, that state will I shortly declare to thee.

He who controls all the doors (of the senses), staying the mind in the heart, fixing his breath in the head, established in the holding still of Yoga,

Repeating OM, the one syllable, Brahma, and thinking on me, when he goes forth abandoning a body, he goes the highest way.

By the Yogi, ever trained, whose mind is never elsewhere, who thinks ever on me, I am easily reached, O son of Pṛithā.

15. They who have come to me, the great-souled ones, go not to rebirth, the impermanent place of pain; they have gone to the highest state.

The worlds from the heaven of Brahma again return, O Arjuna; but he who has come to me, O son of Kuntī, finds not birth again.

In that they know a day of Brahma of a thousand ages, and a night of a thousand ages, they are those who know day and night.

From the unmanifested all manifestations proceed at the coming of day; when night comes, they are dissolved even into that which is named the unmanifested.

Even this host of beings arises again and again, and is dissolved without its will at the coming of night, O son of Pṛithā, and when day comes it is produced.

20. But beyond that there is another being, unmanifested, eternal, beyond the manifested, which when all beings perish, perishes not.

The unmanifested, the indestructible it is called; they call it the supreme way. When they have attained it, they return not. This is my supreme abode.

This is the highest Person, O son of Pṛithā, to be gained by undivided devotion, wherein beings abide, and by whom all this has been created.

But what that time is, when Yogis on their departure go forth not to return, or to return again, that will I declare, O best of Bharatas.

Fire, light, day, the bright half of the month, the six months of the sun's northern path, if at those times they depart, the knowers of Brahma go to Brahma.

25. Likewise smoke, night, the dark half of the month, the six months of the sun's southern path, at those times the Yogi attains the moonlight and returns.

For these light and dark ways are held to be the eternal paths of the world; by the former he goes to return not, by the other he returns again.

The Yogi knowing these paths, O son of Pṛithā, is in no way bewildered; therefore at all times be trained in Yoga, O Arjuna.[1]

The fruit of merit declared in the Vedas, in sacrifices, in austerities, and in almsgivings, the Yogi knowing all this passes beyond it, and reaches the highest, primal abode.

[1] This passage, 23–27, has been held to be a late addition, but it is simply repeating the teaching found in several Upanishads (*Bṛihadār.*, vi, 2, 15; *Chānd.*, v, 10, 1; *Praśna*, i, 4, 9). The Mahābhārata itself tells how Bhīshma, when fatally wounded in the battle, practised Yoga and postponed his death, so that he might die at the auspicious time when the sun was in its northern course between the winter and the summer solstices.

IX

THE ROYAL KNOWLEDGE AND SECRET

The Lord reveals the secret of his nature as creator and supporter of the universe and as the true object of worship.

BUT I will tell to thee, who art without ill-will, this most secret knowledge and understanding, by knowing which thou wilt here be released from evil;

This royal knowledge, this royal secret, this highest means of purification, to be understood at sight, righteous, easy to perform, and changeless.

Men who believe not in this righteousness, O hero, attain not to me; they attain to the path of death and rebirth.

By me in the form of the unmanifested has all this universe been created; all beings abide in me, but I abide not in them.

5. Yet beings abide not in me; behold the Yoga of me the Lord. I bear these things, yet I abide not in beings; my own self is the abode of beings.[1]

As the great wind, ever established in space,

[1] The Lord as Nature is the material cause of the world, and hence is immanent; but he is also transcendent.

goes everywhere, so all beings abide in me: thus understand it.

All beings, O son of Kuntī, go to my Nature at the end of a world-cycle, and again at the beginning of a cycle I emit them.

Resting on my Nature again and again I emit this whole host of beings without their choice, through the power of my Nature.

Yet these actions bind me not, O Dhananjaya; as one impartial I sit not attached to these actions.

10. With me as overseer Nature produces that which moves and that which moves not. It is through this cause, O son of Kuntī, that the world revolves.

They despise me when I have taken my abode in a human body—the bewildered, who know not my highest nature as Lord of beings.

Vain is their hope, vain their actions, vain their knowledge, mindless ones; it is on the demonic and undivine bewildering Nature that they depend.

But those of great soul, O son of Pṛithā, depending upon my divine Nature, worship me with single minds, knowing me as the changeless origin of beings.

Ever praising me, and striving firm in their vows, revering me with devotion, ever trained they worship me.

15. And others, sacrificing with the sacrifice of

knowledge worship me as one or as several, in many ways—so they worship me, who face every way.

I am the oblation, I am the sacrifice, the offering to the fathers am I; I am the herb, the sacred formula; I am also the melted butter, I am the fire, I am the burnt offering.

I am the father of this universe, the mother, the supporter, the grandfather, that which should be known, the purifier, OM, the Rigveda, the Sāmaveda, the Yajurveda[1];

The way, the supporter, the Lord, the witness, the abode, the refuge, the friend, the origin, the dissolution, the abiding-place, the storehouse, the changeless seed.

I give heat, I hold back the rain and send it forth; I am the immortal and also death; being and non-being am I, O Arjuna.

20. They who know the three Vedas, the drinkers of the Soma, purified from sin, who offer sacrifices, desire the way to heaven; they win the holy world of the king of the gods, and eat the divine feasts of the gods in heaven.

When they have enjoyed the spacious world of heaven, they enter the world of mortals when their merit is exhausted; even so following the threefold righteousness, with desire for desires they obtain going and coming.

[1] The Veda of hymns, the Veda of chants, and the Veda which besides hymns contains sacrificial formulas.

They who thinking on me with single mind worship me, who are ever trained, to them I bring the gaining of peace.[1]

They too who are devoted to other gods, who offer sacrifice endowed with faith, also worship me, O son of Kuntī, though not according to ancient precept.

For I am the enjoyer and the Lord of all sacrifices; but they know me not in reality, and hence they fall (to another birth).

25. They who are vowed to the gods go to the gods, those vowed to the fathers to the fathers; they who sacrifice to nature-spirits to the nature-spirits, but worshippers of me go to me.

If one with devotion offers me a leaf, a flower, a fruit, or water, that offering made with devotion I accept from the striving soul.

Whatever thou doest, or eatest, or sacrificest, or givest, whatever thy austerity, O son of Kuntī, do that as dedicated to me.

Thus from the fruits of good and evil shalt thou be released, from the bonds of action; with thy self trained by the Yoga of renunciation thou shalt be freed and come to me.

I am of even mind towards all beings; none is

[1] *Yogakshema.* This is a word with a long history, which has changed its meaning more than once. In II, 45, it is something to be avoided, and there means, according to Śankara, the protecting of what has been gained. In Buddhist texts it means nirvāṇa, and probably has that meaning here in the sense of final goal.

hateful to me nor dear; but they who worship me with devotion are in me and I in them.

30. Even if he is a very evil liver, but worships me with single devotion, he must be held good, for he has rightly resolved.

Quickly he becomes of righteous soul, and goes to eternal peace. O son of Kuntī, understand this: no one devoted to me is destroyed.

For those who resort to me, O son of Pṛithā, though of base birth—women, vaiśyas and śūdras,[1] they too go the highest way.

How much more pious brahmins and devoted royal sages; thou hast attained this impermanent, joyless world, yet worship me.

Set thy mind on me, be devoted to me, sacrifice to me, reverence me; to me shalt thou come, if thou trainest thyself, and holdest me as the goal.

X

THE LORD'S VASTNESS

The Lord now reveals his nature as comprehending all existences, and as immanent in them and constituting the reality of each.

THE Lord said: Hear further, O mighty-armed, my supreme utterance, which I will tell thee, who delightest therein, for I wish thy good.

[1] See note on XVIII, 41.

Neither the host of gods nor the great sages know my source ; for I am entirely the beginning of the gods and great sages.

He who knows me as the unborn, the beginningless, the Lord of the world, he unbewildered among mortals is freed from all sins.

Intellect, knowledge, absence of bewilderment, patience, truth, self-control, calm, pleasure and pain, becoming, non-being, fear and bravery,

5. Non-injuring, equanimity, contentment, austerity, almsgiving, fame and ill-fame, are the separate kinds that arise from me.

The seven great sages, the ancient four, and likewise the Manus[1] were mind-born from my nature, and from them is this offspring in the world.

He who knows in truth this vastness and Yoga of mine is trained by unshaken Yoga ; of this there is no doubt.

I am the source of all ; from me everything arises ; so deeming the wise worship me endowed with my nature.

With their minds on me, their life-breath dedicated to me, they enlighten one another ; and ever conversing about me they are content and happy.

10. To those who are ever trained, and who

[1] Manu is the first man at the beginning of each new race of beings. The four are four ancient sages.

worship with affection, I give the Yoga of the intellect, through which they come to me.

In order to show compassion on them I abide in their selves, and destroy the darkness born of ignorance with the shining lamp of knowledge.

Arjuna said: The supreme Brahma, the supreme abode, the highest purifier art thou; the Person, eternal, divine, the first of gods, the unborn, the Lord.

Thus all the sages speak of thee, and likewise the divine sage Nārada; Asita, Devala, and Vyāsa, and thou too tellest me.

All this I deem to be true which thou tellest me, O Keśava; for neither the gods nor the Dānavas,[1] O Lord, know thy manifestation.

15. Thou verily knowest thyself by thyself, O highest Person, abode of beings, Lord of beings, God of gods, ruler of the world.

Deign then to tell in full thy divine vastnesses, through which thou abidest enveloping these worlds.

How by ever thinking may I know thee, O Yogi? And in what natures may I think upon thee, O Lord?

Tell more and at length of thy Yoga and thy vastness, O Janārdana; for I am never sated with hearing the immortal (teaching).

[1] Supernatural beings hostile to the gods, reckoned as a class of asuras; the Daityas (V, 30) are another class. For the myth of the asuras see XVI.

The Lord said: Come, I will tell thee, for divine are my vastnesses, O best of Kurus; the chief (I will tell), for there is no end to my extent.

20. I am the self, O Guḍākeśa, abiding in the seat of all beings. I am the beginning and the middle of beings, and likewise the end.

Of the Ādityas[1] I am Vishṇu, of lights the gleaming sun, the Marīchi of the Maruts am I, and the moon among the constellations.

Of the Vedas I am the Sāmaveda, of the gods Vāsava (Indra); of the senses I am the mind, and of living creatures consciousness.

Of the Rudras I am Śankara, Vitteśa of the yakshas and rakshases[2]; of the Vasus I am fire, and of mountain peaks Meru.

Of household priests know that I am the foremost, Bṛihaspati, O son of Pṛithā; of generals I am Skanda, of lakes I am the ocean.

25. Of great sages I am Bhṛigu, of invocations the one syllable; of sacrifices am I the sacrifice with muttered utterance, of firm-fixed things I am the Himālaya.

I am the sacred fig tree of all trees, of divine sages Nārada, of the heavenly musicians Chitraratha, of siddhas[3] the ascetic Kapila.

Know me among horses as Uchchaiḥśravas,

[1] A class of seven or eight Vedic gods; the names of the following gods are also Vedic.

[2] Classes of goblin-like spirits.

[3] Those who have attained perfection in this life; Kapila is the traditional author of the Sānkhya philosophy.

born of the drink of immortality [1]; among king-elephants Airāvata, and among men the king.

Of weapons I am the thunderbolt, of cows I am the cow of desires; I am the ancestor Kandarpa, of serpents I am Vāsuki.

I am Ananta of snakes, Varuṇa of water creatures; of the fathers I am Aryaman, I am Yama of restrainers.

30. I am Prahlāda of the Daityas, of calculators Time; of beasts the king of beasts, and Vainateya [2] of birds.

Of purifiers I am the purifying wind, I am Rāma of those that bear weapons; of fishes I am the Makara, of streams I am the Ganges.

Of creations I am the beginning, end, and middle, O Arjuna; of sciences I am the science of the self; I am the speech of speakers.

Of letters I am A, of the compound word I am the copulative,[3] I am also imperishable time; I am the Supporter facing every way.

I am death that seizes all, the origin of all that shall be; of things feminine I am fame, prosperity, speech, memory, wisdom, firmness, and patience.

35. Of the Sāman hymns I am the Bṛihat

[1] When the gods churned the ocean to obtain the drink of immortality, other treasures were produced also, among them the horse and the cow of desires.

[2] Garuḍa, the bird of Vishṇu.

[3] A compound of two nouns, e.g. *pāṇipadam* "hand and foot."

Sāman, of metres I am the Gāyatrī,[1] of months I am Mārgaśīrsha (November–December), of the seasons I am the flowery.

I am the gambling of the cheats, the brilliance of the brilliant; I am victory, I am resolution, I am the goodness of the good.

Of the Vṛishṇis I am Vāsudeva,[2] of the Pāṇḍus Dhananjaya; of recluses I am Vyāsa, of seers the seer Uśanas.

I am the rod of them that subdue, the statecraft of them that desire victory; I am the silence of secrets, the knowledge of the knowers.

Whatever is the seed of all beings that am I, O Arjuna; nor is there a creature that moves or moves not which may exist without me.

40. No end is there of my divine vastnesses, O hero; but this extent of my vastness have I declared by these instances.

Whatever is vast, good, auspicious, or mighty, understand thou that it exists as a portion of my splendour.

Nevertheless, what is this lengthy teaching to thee, O Arjuna? With one portion of myself I have fixed this whole universe, and I abide.

[1] A verse of twenty-four syllables, especially the verse in this metre, recited daily by brahmins, the *Sāvitrī*:

> Upon that excellent glory
> Of God Savitar may we think,
> That he may stimulate our thoughts.

[2] Vṛishṇi was an ancestor in the family of Kṛishṇa Vāsudeva is a name of Kṛishṇa as the son of Vasudeva.

XI

THE LORD AS ALL FORMS

As Arjuna has just been told of the Lord as embracing and forming the essence of all beings, he now wishes to see the form of the Lord as manifested in all beings in the universe, and the vision is granted to him.

ARJUNA said: Since out of kindness to me thou hast declared to me the word of the supreme secret named present in the self, thereby my bewilderment is gone from me.

For I have heard at length from thy very self of the rising and passing away of beings, O lotus-eyed, and of thy changeless majesty.

Even as thou dost tell of thyself, O supreme Lord, so do I desire to behold thy form as Lord, O highest Person.

If thou deemest that I am able to behold it, O Lord, then, O Lord of Yoga, show me thy changeless self.

5. The Lord said: Behold, O son of Pṛithā, my hundredfold and thousandfold forms, my manifold forms, divine and of many colours and shapes.

Behold the Ādityas, the Vasus, the Rudras, the Aśvins, and likewise the Maruts, and many marvellous forms never seen before, O Bhārata.

Behold now the entire world of that which moves and that which moves not standing here in my body, O Guḍākeśa, and whatever else thou hast a wish to see.

But thou art unable to behold me with thy own eye; a divine eye I give thee: behold the Yoga of me as Lord.

Sanjaya said: As he thus spake, O king, then Hari, the great Lord of Yoga, showed to the son of Pṛithā his supreme form as Lord.

10. With many mouths and eyes, showing many wonders, with many divine adornments and many divine weapons upraised;

Wearing divine garlands and robes, with divine scents and unguents, all marvellous was this God, infinite, facing every way.

If in the heavens the splendour of a thousand suns all together should blaze out, like that would be the splendour of that great-souled one.

There the son of Pāṇḍu then saw in one the whole world manifoldly divided in the body of the God of gods.

Thereat filled with amazement, with hair on end, Dhananjaya bowed down his head, and clasping his hands addressed the God.

15. Arjuna said:

I see all gods, O God, within thy body,
And likewise all the various hosts of beings,
Brahmā the Lord on lotus-throne abiding,
The sages all, and all the snakes of heaven.

With countless arms and mouths and eyes and bodies
Thee I behold, all round in forms unnumbered ;
Of thee no end, no middle, no beginning
I see, O Lord of all, all forms possessing.

Bearing the diadem, the mace, the discus,
Shining all round about, a mass of glory,
Thee I behold, hard to be seen, yet shining
Like fire or sun all round, immeasurable.

The eternal thou, the supreme point of knowledge,
Thou of this all the highest place of treasure,
The changeless thou, guard of eternal duty,
The everlasting Person, so I deem thee.

Without beginning, middle, end, unending
Thy power, thy arms, the sun and moon thy eyes,
Thee I behold with mouth of gleaming fire ;
With thy own blaze this universe thou heatest.

20. The space twixt heaven and earth is all enveloped
By thee alone, and so are all the quarters ;
Seeing this wondrous form of thine, so dreadful,
The triple world, O mighty Soul, is shaken.

To thee the gods with their assemblies enter ;
Some terrified with folded hands extol thee,
Crying all hail ; great seers and troops of siddhas
Praise thee with their abundant hymns of praises.

Rudras, Ādityas, Vasus, and the Sādhyas,
All-gods and Aśvins, Maruts, and the fathers,
Gandharvas, Yakshas, Asuras, and Siddhas
Assembled all behold thee with amazement.
Thy mighty form with many mouths beholding,
O mighty-armed, with eyes, arms, thighs, and feet,
With many bellies, and many dreadful fangs,
The worlds all tremble, even as I do also.
Touching the clouds, blazing with many colours,
Thy open mouths I see, thy wide eyes blazing ;
Beholding thee my inner being trembles,
No firmness do I find, no rest, O Vishṇu.
25. Thy mouths with many dreadful fangs beholding,
Like to Time's universal conflagration,
I know the quarters not, I find no shelter,
Be gracious, Lord of gods, the world's protection.
And also all those sons of Dhṛitarāshṭra
Together with these hosts of world-protectors,
Bhīshma, Droṇa, the charioteer's son Karṇa,
With our own warriors, our chiefest fighters,
Are hasting, hurrying thy mouths to enter,
Furnished with dreadful fangs and fear-inspiring ;
Some of them caught upon thy teeth are fastened,
There they are seen, their heads are crushed between them.
Like as the streams of water of the rivers
Flow ever rushing downwards to the ocean,

So likewise these world-heroes, moving onward,
Into thy blazing mouths they rush and enter.
As moths in rapid flight too swiftly rushing
A blazing flame to their destruction enter,
So do the worlds in flight too swiftly rushing
Into thy mouths to their destruction enter.
30. Thou lickest up and swallowest entirely
The worlds around, with blazing mouths devouring;
The entire universe with light thou fillest;
The dreadful rays of thine blaze forth, O Vishṇu.
Tell me, O thou of dreadful form, who art thou?
Reverence to thee, O best of gods, be gracious;
I fain would understand thy primal nature,
For thy appearing thus I know not.
The Lord said:
Know I am Time, that makes the worlds to perish,
When ripe, and come to bring on them destruction;
Even without thee they all shall cease their being,
Who stand arrayed in hostile ranks as warriors.
Therefore arise, stand up, and win thou glory,
Defeat thy foes; enjoy successful kingship;
Even by me these men are slain already;
Be but the means, right and left-handed archer.

Droṇa and Bhīshma too and Jayadratha,
Karṇa likewise, and other warrior heroes
Slain now by me, slay thou, and do not tremble;
Fight; in the fray thy rivals thou shalt conquer.

35. Sanjaya said: Hearing these words of Keśava, the wearer of the diadem (Arjuna) clasped his hands trembling, did reverence, and spoke further to Kṛishṇa, stammering with fear and making obeisance.

Arjuna said:

Rightly, O Hṛishīkeśa, at thy praises
The universe is gladdened and rejoices;
The rakshases in terror flee to all quarters,
And all the hosts of siddhas do thee reverence.

And wherefore should they not to thee do reverence,
Great-souled one, greater than Brahmā, first creator?
O infinite Lord of gods, the world's home art thou,
The imperishable, being, non-being, and beyond them.

Thou art the primal God, the ancient Person,
Thou of this all the supreme place of treasure,
Knower and knowable, the supreme dwelling,
Boundless of form, by thee is all created.

Vāyu and Varuṇa, fire, moon, and Yama,
Prajāpati art thou, the fathers' father;
Reverence, reverence to thee a thousandfold,

And yet again to thee be reverence, reverence.
40. Reverence before thee, reverence behind thee,
O All, to thee be reverence from all sides ;
O endless in thy strength, boundless in vigour,
All thou envelopest, all therefore art thou.

Deeming thee friend, whate'er I have uttered roughly,
Calling thee Kṛishṇa, Yādava, or comrade,
Whate'er, not knowing aught of this thy greatness,
Speaking in carelessness or in affection,

Whate'er in jest I have spoken with irreverence,
When in our sports, or resting, or in eating,
Alone, in other's presence, O firm-fixéd,
For that I crave thee pardon, boundless one.

Father of all the world that moves and moves not
Art thou, and worshipful most reverend teacher ;
None is like thee, much less is there a greater
In the three worlds ; thy glory has no equal.

Therefore I bow, and casting down my body
I seek thy favour, Lord adorable ;
As father spares his son, comrade his comrade,
As friend his friend,[1] so do thou deign to spare me.

[1] Śankara treats this word as feminine. Mr. M. M. Bose thinks that it shows the development in Śankara's time of the sexualism of later schools. See *The Post-Caitanya Sahajiā Cult of Bengal*, p. 146, Calcutta, 1930.

45. With ecstasy have I beheld what no one
Has seen before ; with fear my mind is shaken ;
Therefore, O God, show me thy other body ;
Be gracious, Lord of gods, the world's one refuge.
Holding the diadem, the mace, the discus,
As erst thou wert, so do I wish to see thee.
That very form, four-armed one, take upon thee,
O thousand-armed, O figure universal.
The Lord said :
Favour to thee, O Arjuna, have I granted,
Showing my highest form through this my Yoga ;
Glorious, entire, and infinite and primal,
Except by thee ne'er seen before by any.
Not by the Vedas, sacrifices, studies,
Or alms, or ritual, or by gruesome penance
Can I like that be seen in the world of creatures,
Except by thee, O hero of the Kurus.
Tremble thou not, be not thyself bewildered
At thus this awful form of mine beholding ;
Cast away fear, and with thy heart rejoicing
Once more behold that form beheld aforetime.

50. Sanjaya said : Even so Vāsudeva having thus spoken to Arjuna showed once more his own body ; and the great-souled one consoled him in his terror, assuming his gentle form again.

Arjuna said : On seeing this gentle, human

form of thine, O Janārdana, I now have become collected, and have come to my natural state.

The Lord said : Very hard to see is that form of mine which thou hast beheld. Even the gods ever long to behold that form.

Not through the Vedas or austerity, not through almsgiving or sacrifice can I be seen thus, as thou hast seen me.

But by single devotion, O Arjuna, can I be thus known and seen in reality and entered, O hero.

55. Who does my action, who makes me his aim, who is devoted to me, free from attachment, without hatred to any being, he comes to me, O son of Pāṇḍu.[1]

XII

DEVOTION

The Lord explains the best way in which he may be worshipped, and who is the best worshipper.

ARJUNA said : Then of those devotees who ever trained worship thee, and of those who worship the imperishable, the unmanifested, which are the best knowers of Yoga ?

[1] This verse is called by Śankara " the essence of the whole Gītā-śāstra."

The Lord said: They who place their minds in me, and constantly trained worship me, endowed with supreme faith, I deem to be the best trained.

But they who worship the imperishable, the undesignable, the unmanifested, the all-present, the unthinkable, the unshakable, the immovable, the stable,

Restraining the troop of senses everywhere, with balanced intellect, they too attain to me, delighting in the good of all beings.[1]

5. Greater is the trouble of those whose minds are attached to the unmanifested; for the unmanifested way involves embodied ones in pain.

But those who renounce all actions in me, who are intent on me, who meditate on me with single Yoga, and worship me,

Those do I lift up quickly from the ocean of death and rebirth, O son of Pṛithā, whose minds are placed in me.

Set thy mind on me, place thy intellect in me; in me verily shalt thou dwell hereafter, there is no doubt.

In case thou canst not concentrate thy mind firmly on me, then by the Yoga of exercise seek to reach me, O Dhananjaya.

10. Even if thou art unable to perform exercise,

[1] Both these classes worship the One, the imperishable, but the former are those who know that the One is the Lord.

be intent on doing my action; even in doing actions for my sake thou wilt attain success.

If thou art unable to do even this, depending on my Yoga, then abandon the fruit of all action with restrained self.

For better is knowledge than exercise, meditation than knowledge, abandonment of the fruit of action than meditation; close upon abandonment follows peace.[1]

He who is without hatred to any being, who is friendly and compassionate, not thinking of mine or myself, balanced in pleasure and pain, patient,

Who is ever content, practising Yoga, with his self restrained, his conviction firm, his mind and intellect dedicated to me, devoted to me, that man is dear to me.

15. He from whom the world does not shrink away, and who shrinks not away from the world, who is free from elation, impatience, fear, and shrinking, he too is dear to me.

He who looks for nothing, who is pure, prompt, impartial, free from trembling, who has abandoned all undertakings, who is devoted to me, that man is dear to me.

[1] The abandonment of actions is best, since when done completely it brings to the goal. Meditation is lower, for it is only a means. Knowledge, in the sense of knowledge of what the goal is, is lower still, for meditation has not yet began, and still lower is exercise, which may be begun without any knowledge of the true goal.

He who exults not nor hates, nor sorrows, nor longs, who has abandoned good and bad, full of devotion, that man is dear to me.

He who is the same to foe and friend, honour and dishonour, who is the same in cold and heat, pleasure and pain, and is without attachment,

Who holds blame and praise equal, silent, content with anything, without a home, of firm thought and full of devotion, to me that man is dear.

But they who worship this righteous immortal (teaching), as I have uttered it, full of faith, making me their supreme object, devoted, they to me are surpassingly dear.

XIII

THE FIELD AND THE KNOWER OF THE FIELD

The distinction between Nature and the self is expounded, Nature being the evolution not merely of the material world and the human body, but also of the mental faculties and all the changing phenomena of thought and feeling. Behind all this is the unchanging self as a spectator. The self is deluded when it thinks it is an actor in these changes. To attain knowledge of the distinction is to perceive the self and hence also the highest self.

THE Lord said: This body, O son of Kuntī, is called the field, and that which knows it is called by knowers thereof the knower of the field.[1]

Also understand me as the knower of the field in all fields, O Bhārata; knowledge of the field and of the knower, that is knowledge indeed, I deem.

What the field is, and what it is like, what its changes are, whence it is, and what he (the knower) is and his power, that hear from me in brief.

It has been sung by sages in many ways, in various different chants, and also in the words of the Brahma-sūtras[2] furnished with reasonings and decisions.

5. The great elements, the thought of I, intellect, the unmanifested, the ten senses and the one (mind), and the five fields of the senses,

Wish, hate, pleasure, pain, combination (of the bodily organs), consciousness, firmness—this is the field with its changes related in brief.

Humility, honesty, non-injury, patience, up-

[1] Some MSS. insert the following as the first verse: Arjuna said: Nature and the Person, the field and the knower of the field, this I wish to know, and also knowledge and that which should be known, O Keśava.

[2] This is the name of the authoritative work of the Vedānta system, in which the principles are stated in sūtras (short aphoristic statements), but these sūtras as we now possess them mention Buddhist and other doctrines certainly later than the Song. The name Vedānta, "end of the Vedas," probably existed earlier than the system as a name for the teaching of the Upanishads, as in XV, 15.

rightness, service to the teacher, purity, steadfastness, self-restraint,

Absence of passion for the objects of sense, absence of the thought of I, insight into the evils of birth, death, old age, sickness, and pain,

Unattachment, absence of clinging to children, wife, and possessions, constant evenness of mind towards desired and undesired events,

10. Devotion to me with single Yoga without going astray, resorting to lonely places, dislike for the company of men,

Constancy in the knowledge of that present in the self, insight into the object of the knowledge of the real—this has been declared to be knowledge. Ignorance is that which is otherwise than this.

What that which should be known is I will declare, by knowing which one enjoys the immortal: the beginningless, supreme Brahma, called neither being nor non-being.

Having everywhere hands and feet, everywhere eyes, head, and mouth, everywhere hearing, it abides in the world enveloping everything.

Appearing with the constituents of all the senses, but free from all the senses, unattached and supporting all, not possessing constituents, yet enjoying the constituents,

15. Outside and inside beings, moving and moving not, through its subtlety imperceptible, abiding far away and yet within is that.

Not divided among beings, and yet remaining as if distributed, supporter of beings is that which should be known; it constantly devours and generates.

The light of lights, beyond the darkness it is called, knowledge, that which should be known, approachable by knowledge, seated in the heart of everyone.

So the field, and likewise knowledge and that which should be known have been shortly told. My devotee understanding this is fitted for my being.

Know that Nature and the Person are both without beginning; know that changes and the constituents arise from Nature.

20. Nature is called the causer in the production of effects and causes; the Person is called the causer of the enjoyment of pleasures and pains.

For the Person abiding in Nature enjoys the constituents originating from Nature. His attachment to the constituents is the cause of his being born in bad and good births.

Spectator, approver, supporter, enjoyer, the great Lord, the highest self—thus is called the supreme Person in the body.

He who thus knows the Person and Nature with its constituents, in whatever way he exists, is not born again.

By meditation on the self some see the self

through the self, some by the Yoga of Sānkhya, and others by the Yoga of action.[1]

25. But others not thus knowing, worship by hearing from others ; they also pass beyond death, intent on what they have heard.

Whatever creature is born, which moves not or moves, know that it is through the union of the knower of the field with the field, O best of Bharatas.

The highest Lord that abides evenly in all beings, that perishes not in the perishable—he who sees him sees.

For as he sees the Lord everywhere abiding equally, he destroys not the self through the self ; hence he goes the highest way.

And he who sees that actions are done in every way by Nature, and thus the self as a non-actor, he sees.

30. When he sees the separate existence of beings abiding in one, and its extension thence, then he attains to Brahma.

Through being without beginning, without constituents, this supreme changeless self, even when abiding in the body, O son of Kuntī, acts not and is stained not.

As all-pervading space through its subtlety is

[1] The three methods of reaching the goal are here referred to as Yoga ; Yoga-practice proper, the Sānkhya method of reflecting on the distinction between the self and Nature, and the method of abandoning the fruit of actions.

not stained, so the self, which abides everywhere in the body, is not stained.

As the one sun illumines this whole world, so the dweller in the field illumines the whole field, O Bhārata.

Even so they who know the difference between the field and the knower of the field with the eye of knowledge, and release of beings from Nature, go to the Supreme.

XIV

DISTINCTION OF THE THREE CONSTITUENTS

The Lord again shows how beings are born, and what their different types are according as the constituent of goodness, passion, or dullness predominates in their characters, and what freedom from contact with the constituents means.

THE Lord said: Again will I proclaim the highest of knowledges, the supreme knowledge, by knowing which all recluses have gone hence to the highest state.

By resorting to this knowledge and coming to be of my nature, even when the universe is created they are not reborn, nor do they tremble at a destruction of it.

My womb is the great Brahma; therein I place the germ; thence is the arising of all beings, O Bhārata.

Whatever forms arise in any wombs, O son of Kuntī, the great Brahma is their womb. I am the father who gives the seed.

5. Goodness, passion, and dullness are the constituents that arise from Nature; they bind the changeless embodied one in the body, O great-armed one.

Of these goodness through its spotlessness is bright and healthy; it binds through attachment to pleasure and through attachment to knowledge, O sinless one.

Know that passion, being of passionate nature, arises through attachment to craving; it binds the embodied one, O son of Kuntī, through attachment to action.

But know that dullness, born of ignorance, is the bewilderment of all embodied ones; it binds through negligence, laziness, and sloth, O Bhārata.

Goodness attaches to pleasure, passion to action, O Bhārata; but dullness envelops knowledge and attaches to negligence.

10. Goodness may get the mastery over passion and dullness, O Bhārata, passion over goodness and dullness, and likewise dullness over goodness and passion.

When through all the doors in the body the

light of knowledge appears, then should it be known that goodness has increased.

Greed, activity, undertaking of actions, restlessness, desire—these appear when passion has increased, O best of Bharatas.

Darkness, inactivity, negligence, and bewilderment—these appear when dullness has increased, O son of the Kurus.

But if the embodied one goes to dissolution (death) when goodness has increased, then he goes to the spotless worlds of the knowers of the highest.

15. If in passion he goes to dissolution, he is reborn among those attached to action; likewise if in dullness, he is reborn among those of bewildered birth.

They say that the fruit of a well-done action is full of goodness and spotless; but the fruit of passion is pain, and ignorance is the fruit of dullness.

From goodness knowledge is born, and from passion greed; from dullness arise negligence and bewilderment and also ignorance.

They who abide in goodness go upwards, the passionate stand in the middle; the dull abiding in the state of the lowest constituent go downwards.

When the seer perceives that there is no other actor than the constituents, and knows that which is beyond the constituents, he attains to my nature.

20. When the embodied one has passed beyond these three constituents which are the origin of bodies, freed from birth, death, old age, and pain he enjoys the immortal.

Arjuna said: What marks are his who has passed beyond the three constituents, O Lord? What is his conduct, and how does he go beyond these three constituents?

The Lord said: He hates not brightness, nor activity, nor even bewilderment, O son of Pāṇḍu, when they have come forth, nor does he long for them when they have departed.

He who sits as one neutral, and is not shaken by the constituents, saying "the constituents move about," who stays and moves not,

In whom pleasure and pain are the same, who stays in himself, to whom a clod, a stone, and gold are the same, to whom the pleasant and unpleasant are equal, who is firm, to whom blame and praise are equal,

25. Who is equal in honour and dishonour, equal towards parties of friends and foes, and who has abandoned all undertakings, he is said to have passed beyond the constituents.

And he who without going astray serves me with the Yoga of devotion goes beyond these constituents, and is fit to become Brahma.

I am the abode of Brahma, the immortal, the changeless, of eternal righteousness, and of absolute happiness.

XV

THE LORD AS THE HIGHEST PERSON

The universe of birth and death is represented as a tree. The cutting of it down means achieving complete non-attachment to the things of sense, whereby rebirth ceases. The soul is a portion of the Lord behind all physical and psychical phenomena. The immanence of the Lord is again declared.

WITH roots above and branches below, the sacred fig-tree,[1] they say, is unchanging; its leaves are the verṣes. He who knows this knows the Vedas.

Downwards and upwards stretch its branches growing from the constituents; its shoots are the objects of sense. Downwards its roots extend, resulting in action in the world of men.

Its form thus described is not here grasped, nor its end, nor its beginning, nor its present state. By cutting down this strongly rooted fig-tree with the firm axe of non-attachment,

Then is the place to be sought, to which when men have gone they return not from it

[1] This is the *aśvattha*, the pīpal, *Ficus religiosa*. It is not likely that the author confused it with the *nyagrodha*, the banyan, *Ficus indica*, which sends roots down from its branches. This is an inverted tree, and the image is taken from *Kaṭha Up*. vi, 1, where it means "Brahma, the immortal," but here it is the world of rebirth (*saṁsāra*), which is to be cut down by attaining complete severance from it.

again; and to that primal Person one goes, from whom the ancient activity (of creation) has issued.

5. Free from pride and bewilderment, the vice of attachment conquered, ever contemplating the present in the self, with desires stayed, freed from the pairs called pleasure and pain, they go unbewildered to that changeless place.

Neither sun nor moon nor fire lightens that place to which when they have gone they return not, that supreme abode of mine.

A portion even of me, which becoming an immortal living being in the world of living beings, draws together the senses with mind as the sixth existing in Nature.

When the Lord (the soul) acquires a body, and when it departs from it, it takes these senses and goes, like the wind taking scents from their receptacle.

It presides over ear, eye, touch, taste, smell, and also the mind, and uses the objects of the senses.

10. When it gets up or stays or enjoys in company with the constituents, the bewildered perceive it not; they who have the eye of knowledge perceive it.

Yogis who are striving perceive it as abiding in themselves; those of untrained selves, even though they strive, perceive it not, the mindless ones.

That brilliance which in the sun illumines the whole world, that in the moon, and that in fire, know that that brilliance is mine.

I enter the earth and support beings with my energy; I nourish all plants, becoming Soma rich in juice.

Becoming the fire of digestion I resort to the bodies of living beings; united with the out-breath and the in-breath I digest food of the four kinds.

15. And I abide in the heart of everyone; from me are memory, knowledge, and their absence. I am that which is to be known by all the Vedas; the maker of the Vedānta[1] and the knower of the Vedas am I.

These two Persons are in the world, the destructible and the indestructible. The destructible is all beings; standing unshakable is the indestructible called.

But the highest Person is another, declared to be the supreme self, who enters the threefold world and supports it, the changeless Lord.

Since I am beyond the destructible, and most high above the indestructible, hence am I in the world and the Veda proclaimed the highest Person.

He who even thus unbewildered knows me as the highest Person, he knowing all worships me with his whole being, O Bhārata.

[1] Or, the maker of the end of the Vedas; see note on XIII, 4.

20. Thus has this most secret doctrine (śāstra) been uttered by me, O sinless one; if one understands this he has intelligence, and has done what has to be done, O Bhārata.

XVI

DISTINCTION OF THE GODLY AND THE UNGODLY

Two types of character are described, that of the virtuous and that of evildoers. The terms are taken from the myth of the devas and asuras. The latter were a class of gods who quarrelled with the devas about the drink of immortality, and were driven from heaven. But they do not represent the principle of evil, nor do they live in the hells. They are among the gods who, in XI, 22, come to worship the Lord. There is no reference in the Song to the events of the myth, and it is clear that the characters described in this chapter are exactly the godly and ungodly.

THE Lord said: Fearlessness, purity of the individual, steadfastness in the Yoga of knowledge, almsgiving, self-control, sacrifice, scripture-study, austerity, uprightness,

Non-injury, truth, freedom from anger, renunciation, peace, absence of slander, compassion towards creatures, absence of greed, mildness, modesty, constancy,

Energy, patience, firmness, purity, harmlessness, and non-arrogance become his who is born to a godly state, O Bhārata.

Hypocrisy, pride, arrogance, anger, harshness, and ignorance are his who is born to an ungodly state.

5. The godly state is deemed to tend to release, the ungodly to bondage; grieve not, for thou wast born to a godly state, O son of Pāṇḍu.

There are two creations of beings in the world, the godly and the ungodly; the godly has been told at length; listen to me of the ungodly, O son of Pṛithā.

The ungodly know not of action that leads to the goal or the reverse [1]; nor is purity or even good conduct or truth found among them.

The world is without reality, without a basis, they say, and without a Lord; not produced by combination of one thing with another,[2] and having only lust as its cause.

Maintaining this view, with corrupted selves, of little intellect, and of fierce deeds, they are born for the destruction of the world as enemies.

10. Indulging in unsatiable desire, full of hypocrisy, pride, and arrogance, through their

[1] This is Śankara's interpretation. The terms usually refer to the evolution and dissolution of the world, but the ethical sense is more probable in this context, as also in XVIII, 30.

[2] That the world in its evolution from Nature is produced by such combination is the Sānkhya view.

bewilderment making false resolves, they engage in action with impure intentions.

Giving themselves up to immense care, which ends only with death, they regard enjoyment of desires as the highest aim, certain that this is all.

Bound by a hundred snares of hope, intent on lust and anger, they strive to obtain wrongly hoards of wealth for indulging in their desires.

" This have I gained to-day ; that wish I shall attain ; this wealth too is mine, and it shall be again in the future."

" I have slain that enemy, and I shall slay others. I am a Lord, an enjoyer, a successful one, strong and happy."

15. " I am wealthy and well-born ; who else is like me ? I will sacrifice, I will give alms, I will rejoice." Thus they say, bewildered by ignorance.

Confused with many thoughts they are involved in the net of bewilderment ; clinging to the enjoyment of desires they fall into foul hell.

Self-conceited, stubborn, full of the pride and intoxication of wealth, they perform sacrifices in name with hypocrisy, not according to precept.

They are given up to selfishness, violence, pride, lust and anger ; and hating me in their own and others' bodies they are ill-willed.

Haters, cruel, the lowest of men in the world of

change, I incessantly throw these impure ones into ungodly births.

20. They reach an ungodly birth, and from birth to birth are bewildered; they attain not to me, O son of Kuntī, and then they go the lowest way.

Threefold is the gate of hell that destroys the self: lust, anger, and greed. Therefore should one abandon these three.

A man, O son of Kuntī, freed from these three gates of darkness, acts for the bettering of his self, and hence he goes the highest way.

He who casts away the rule of the śāstras,[1] following the impulse of desire, attains not success nor happiness nor the highest way.

Therefore be the śāstra thy standard of what ought or ought not to be done, and knowing what has been said of the precept of the śāstras so do action.

[1] The śāstras are "teaching books," especially the dharma-śāstras giving rules and instruction on ritual, ethics, and religion. The Song speaks of its own teaching as śāstra in XV, 20.

XVII

DISTINCTION OF THE THREE FORMS OF FAITH

The faith of individuals is distinguished according to the predominance in them of one of the three constituents. Their food, sacrifice, alms, and austerity are distinguished in the same way.

ARJUNA said: Of those who reject the precept of the śāstras, but who sacrifice endowed with faith, what is their position? Is it one of goodness, passion, or dullness?

The Lord said: Threefold is the faith of embodied ones; it results from their own natures. It is of goodness, passion, or dullness. Hear of it.

The faith of everyone is in accordance with the individual, O Bhārata. A person consists of faith, and according to what he has faith in, so he is.

Those having the character of goodness sacrifice to the gods, those of passion to yakshas and rakshases; they who sacrifice to the troops of ghosts and nature-spirits have the character of dullness.

5. They who perform gruesome austerity not in accordance with the śāstras, full of hypocrisy and selfishness, together with lust, passion, and violence,

Senseless ones, who torment the host of elements in the body, and me also who abide in the inner body—know that they are of ungodly resolves.

Now the food that is liked by each is of three kinds, and so is their sacrifice, austerity, and almsgiving. Hear their differences.

Foods which increase life, vigour, strength, health, happiness, and cheerfulness, which are tasty, oily, solid, and strengthen the heart, are liked by those of the character of goodness.

Foods which are bitter, sour, salty, very hot, sharp, harsh, burning, which give pain, grief, and sickness, are desired by those of passionate character.

10. That which is stale and has lost its flavour and is putrid, remains and leavings, and what is unfit for sacrifice is the food liked by those of dull character.

The sacrifice in accordance with precept, offered by those who do not long for the fruit, but who fix their minds with the thought, "thus should sacrifice be done," is of the character of goodness.

The sacrifice offered with a view to the fruit, and because of hypocrisy, O best of Bharatas, know that it is of the character of passion.

The sacrifice that is without precept, where there is no distribution of food, which is without sacred formulas and gifts to the priests, and deprived of faith, they declare to be of darkness.

Worship paid to the gods, to the twice-born, to teachers and the wise, purity and uprightness, celibacy and non-injury are called the austerity of the body.

15. Speech which causes no agitation, which is truthful, pleasant, and useful, and the practice of scripture-study are called the austerity of speech.

Graciousness of mind, mildness, silence, self-control, and purity of heart, these are called the austerity of mind.

This threefold austerity, practised with the highest faith by men who long not for the fruit, who are trained, they declare to be of goodness.

The austerity which is practised for the sake of honour, dignity, respect and out of hypocrisy, has been said here to be of passion and unsteady and unstable.

The austerity done through a bewildered decision and with self-torture, or for the sake of outdoing another, is declared to be of darkness.

20. The alms given with the thought that it ought to be given, which is given to one who makes no return, at the right place, the right time, and to a fit person, that alms is deemed to be of the character of goodness.

But the alms given for the sake of receiving a return, or with a view to the fruit, or given with vexation, is deemed to be of the character of passion.

Alms given at the wrong place and time and to unfit persons, with disrespect and contempt, is said to be of the character of dullness.

OM, TAT, SAT is deemed to be the threefold designation of Brahma,[1] and by this were the brahmins, the Vedas, and the sacrifices prescribed of old.

Therefore with the utterance OM acts of sacrifice, almsgiving, and austerity are always begun, as stated in the precepts of those who hold the doctrine concerning Brahma.

25. With the utterance of TAT without a view to the fruit, actions of sacrifice and austerity, and various actions of almsgiving are done by those who long for liberation.

The word SAT is applied in the sense of existence and goodness, and is likewise used in the sense of approved action, O son of Pṛithā.

Steadiness in sacrifice, austerity, and almsgiving is also called SAT, and action for the sake of TAT is also called SAT.

Whatever sacrifice or alms is performed or

[1] These terms are duly explained in the text. *Sat* is literally "existent," *asat* "non-existent." *Tat,* "that," is specially used in the "great utterance" of the Upanishads, *tat tvam asi,* "thou art that," expressing the identity of the individual with Brahma.

austerity exercised without faith is called ASAT, O son of Pṛithā, and it is not, either in the next world or in this.

XVIII

RENUNCIATION

Renunciation of actions and abandonment of the fruit of actions are explained. Next three kinds of knowledge are classed according as one of the three constituents is predominant, and in the same way the triple division of action, the actor, intellect, firmness, pleasure, and duties or rules of action. The duty of Arjuna to fight is reasserted. The greatest secret is that he should be wholly devoted to the Lord. Arjuna declares his doubts gone, and Sanjaya expresses his joy at having heard the dialogue.

ARJUNA said: The truth about renunciation, O mighty-armed, I wish to know, and about abandonment severally, O Hṛishīkeśa, slayer of Keśin.

The Lord said: The giving up of actions that involve desire the sages know as renunciation; the abandonment of the fruit of all actions the wise call abandonment.

Some intelligent ones say that action should be abandoned as bad, and others that the action of sacrifice, alms, and austerity should not be abandoned.

Hear my decision about abandonment, O best of Bharatas ; for abandonment, O tiger of men, is expounded as being threefold.

5. The action of sacrifice, alms, and austerity should not indeed be abandoned but performed ; sacrifice, alms, and austerity are means of purification for the intelligent.

But even those actions should only be done in abandoning attachment and the fruits. This, O son of Pṛithā, is my decided and final judgment.

But renunciation of action that is enjoined is not fitting ; the abandonment of such action through bewilderment is expounded as being of dullness.

When one abandons an action through fear of bodily trouble, thinking it is painful, he makes an abandonment which is of passion, and he does not get the fruit of abandonment.

But when one does an action that is enjoined, thinking it ought to be done, O Arjuna, abandoning attachment and the fruit, that abandonment is deemed to be of goodness.

10. The abandoner pervaded with goodness, wise, with his doubts cut away, hates not an unpleasant action, nor is he attached to a pleasant action.

For an embodied one cannot abandon actions wholly ; but he who abandons the fruit of actions is declared to be an abandoner.

Threefold is the fruit of action, wished for,

unwished for, and mixed, which comes after death for those who have not abandoned; but in no way for those who have renounced.

These five causes, O mighty-armed, understand from me, have been declared in the Sānkhya doctrine for the achieving of all actions.

The support (body), the actor, each organ severally, the various separate activities, and destiny [1] as the fifth.

15. Of action which a man undertakes with his body, speech, or mind, whether proper or the reverse, these are the five causes.

Since this is so, if one looks upon the self alone as the actor, he through his imperfect intellect sees not, the stupid one.

He whose nature has not the thought of I, and whose intellect is not stained, even though he slay all these worlds, slays not nor is he bound.

Knowledge, that which should be known, and the knower, are the threefold stimulus of action. The organ, action, and the actor are the threefold components of action.

Knowledge, action, and the actor are said to be threefold according to the differences of the constituents in reckoning the constituents; in what way hear also about them.

[1] In all human actions there is always an unaccountable element, luck, fate, destiny, providence, which the Hindus call *daiva*, lit. " the divine."

20. That by which one perceives one changeless existence in all beings, the undivided in divided things, know that that knowledge is of the character of goodness.

But the knowledge which knows various existences divided severally through their severalty in all beings, know that that knowledge is of the character of passion.

But that which without referring to the cause is attached to a single effect, as if it were the whole, and is not in accordance with reality, and is insufficient, that knowledge is declared to be of the character of dullness.

Action which is enjoined and is free from attachment, and is done without passion and hate by one who does not wish for the fruit, is said to be of the character of goodness.

But the action which is done by one who wishes for the fruit or with the thought of I, or with great effort, is declared to be of the character of passion.

25. The action which is undertaken without regard to what follows, or to loss, injury, or one's own capacity, and with bewilderment is said to be of the character of dullness.

The actor who is freed from attachment, who speaks not of I, endowed with firmness and energy, and who does not change with success or failure, is said to be of the character of goodness.

The actor who is passionate, wishing for the fruit of action, greedy, harmful, impure, given to elation and sorrow, is declared to be of the character of passion.

The actor who is untrained, common, stubborn, cheating, dishonest, lazy, despondent, and dilatory is said to be of the character of dullness.

Hear the threefold distinction of intellect and firmness according to the constituents, told fully and in detail, O Dhananjaya.

30. The intellect which knows that which leads to the goal and the reverse, that which ought to be done, and that which ought not, fear and fearlessness, bondage and release, that, O son of Pṛithā, is of the character of goodness.

The intellect by which one understands erroneously right and wrong, that which ought to be done, and that which ought not, that, O son of Pṛithā, is of the character of passion.

The intellect enveloped in dullness which thinks right to be wrong, and sees all things reversed, O son of Pṛithā, is of the character of dullness.

The firmness with which one holds firm the activities of the mind, the breath and the senses with unwavering Yoga, O son of Pṛithā, is of the character of goodness.

But the firmness, O Arjuna, with which one with attachment holds firm to right, desire, and wealth, with attachment longing for the fruit, O son of Prithā, is of the character of passion.

35. The firmness with which the stupid one does not give up sleep, fear, sorrow, despair, and elation, O son of Pṛithā, is of the character of dullness.

But now hear from me of pleasure of the three kinds, O best of Bharatas, wherein one by exercising it finds delight and puts an end to pain.

That which at first is like poison, but as it ripens is like the drink of immortality, is called pleasure of the character of goodness, and is produced by the serenity of one's intellect.

The pleasure which by union of the senses with their objects is at first like the drink of immortality, but as it ripens is like poison, is deemed to be of the character of passion.

That pleasure which at first and in what follows is a bewilderment to the self, arising from sleep, laziness, and carelessness, is declared to be the character of dullness.

40. There is no individual on earth nor yet in heaven among the gods that is released from these three constituents born of Nature.

The actions of brahmins, kshatriyas, vaiśyas, and śūdras,[1] O hero, have been distributed accord-

[1] The four castes of priests, warriors, the agricultural and trading class, and the servile class.

ing to the constituents arising from their own natures.

Calm, restraint, austerity, purity, patience, and uprightness, knowledge, understanding, and belief, are the action of a brahmin arising from his own nature.

Heroism, splendour, firmness, skill, not fleeing in battle, almsgiving, the character of a ruler, are the action of a kshatriya arising from his own nature.

Farming, cattle-keeping, and trade are the action of a vaiśya arising from his own nature; and service is the action of a śūdra arising from his own nature.

45. By being satisfied with his proper action a man wins success. Hear how he finds success by staying in his proper action.

By worshipping with his proper action him from whom this world of beings has come forth, and by whom all this has been created, a man finds success.

Better is one's own duty without merit than the duty of another well performed; by doing action prescribed by one's own nature one does not fall into sin.

The action that one is born with, O son of Kuntī, should not be abandoned, even though faulty; for all undertakings are involved in fault as fire by smoke.

He whose intellect is everywhere unattached, whose self is subdued, in whom desire is gone, attains by renunciation to the highest success in freedom from action.

50. How one who has attained success likewise attains Brahma, which is the highest state of knowledge. O son of Kuntī, briefly understand from me.

Trained by purified intellect, and restraining the self by firmness, abandoning sound and the other objects of sense, and giving up passion and hate,

Haunting solitude, eating little, with speech, body, and mind restrained, intent on the Yoga of meditation, and ever resorting to absence of passion,

Free from the thought of I, from violence, pride, desire, anger, possessions, thinking not of mine, and calmed, he is fit to become Brahma.

When he has become Brahma, with serene self, he sorrows not nor longs ; the same to all beings he wins brightest devotion to me.

55. Through devotion he knows me, who and what I am in reality ; then knowing me in reality he enters at once.

And ever performing all actions, taking refuge in me, through my favour he attains the eternal, changeless abode.

With thy mind renouncing all actions on me, intent on me, resorting to the Yoga of the intellect, ever have thy thought on me.

With thy thought on me through my favour thou shalt pass beyond all difficulties ; yet if through thy thought of I thou wilt not listen, thou shalt perish.

Relying on the thought of I, thou thinkest, "I will not fight"; this thy resolve is false; Nature will constrain thee.

60. Bound by thy proper action, O son of Kuntī, which arises from thy own nature, that which through bewilderment thou dost not wish to do thou wilt do without thy will.

The Lord abides in the heart of all beings, O Arjuna, making all beings revolve mounted on a machine [1] by his magic power.

Go even to him as refuge with thy whole being, O Bhārata; through his favour thou shalt win the highest peace, an eternal abode.

Thus has knowledge more secret than the secret been declared to thee by me; examine it fully, and as thou wilt so do.

Listen again to my highest word, the most secret of all: dear art thou to me most surely; therefore I will speak what is for thy good.

65. Have thy mind on me, be devoted to me, sacrifice to me, do reverence to me. To me thou shalt come; what is true I promise; dear art thou to me.

Abandoning all duties [2] come to me, the one

[1] Śankara says, like wooden figures of a puppet-show.

[2] Śankara says that this includes wrong as well as right; it is "beyond good and evil," not because moral distinctions are unreal, but because the devotee has reached a state beyond action.

refuge; I will free thee from all sins; sorrow not.[1]

This is never to be uttered by thee to one without austerity or devotion, or who wishes not to learn, or who is ill-willed towards me.

He who shall declare this highest secret to my devotees, showing supreme devotion to me, shall come to me, there is no doubt.

No one among men shall there be who does an action dearer to me than that, nor one dearer to me than he on the earth.

70. And whoever shall study this our dialogue of righteousness, I shall be worshipped by him with the sacrifice of knowledge, I deem.

The man also who has faith and is not ill-willed, should he hear it, he too is freed, and attains the pure worlds of those who do meritorious actions.

Hast thou heard this, O son of Pṛithā, with thy mind on one point? Is thy ignorance and bewilderment destroyed, O Dhananjaya?

Arjuna said: My bewilderment is destroyed; I have gained memory through thy favour, O stable one. I am established; my doubt is gone; I will do thy word.

Sanjaya said: Thus did I hear the dialogue of Vāsudeva and the great-souled son of Pṛithā, marvellous and causing the hair to rise.

[1] This is called the "final verse" (*carama śloka*), and is looked upon by the school of Rāmānuja as containing the essence of the Song.

75. Through the favour of Vyāsa I heard this supreme secret of Yoga from the Lord of Yoga, Kṛishṇa, himself speaking before my eyes.

O king, as I remember and remember this marvellous dialogue of Keśava and Arjuna, full of merit, I rejoice again and again.

And as I remember and remember that marvellous form of Hari, great is my astonishment, O king, and I rejoice again and again.

Wherever Kṛishṇa, the Lord of Yoga, is, wherever the son of Pṛithā, wielder of the bow, is, there are prosperity, victory, sure welfare, and statecraft, I deem.[1]

SRĪKṚṢṆĀRPAṆAM ASTU

[1] These words make it clear that the meaning of the Song is much more than an incident in an ancient battle. The fight is ever present. Modern Indian thought finds in it an allegorical meaning, much as Dante describes the mystical interpretations of the *Commedia* (Ep. 17). The battlefield Kurukshetra is called *dharmakshetra*, the field of right. There is the Lord, and there is the individual soul, fighting against the distractions of the several senses, till by means of Yoga it attains the light of knowledge.